Help!

For Parents of Children from Ages Three to Six Years

By Parents for Parents

Vol. 4
The Suggestion Circle Series

Edited by
Jean Illsley Clarke,
Marilyn Grevstad,
Sue Hansen,
Mary Paananen, and
Melanie Weiss

1817

Harper & Row, Publishers, San Francisco

Cambridge, Hagerstown, New York, Philadelphia, Washington
London, Mexico City, São Paulo, Singapore, Sydney

To our children, who insist we grow in ways we never imagined we could.

The developmental affirmations for children on pages 14 to 17 are adapted from Pamela Levin's therapeutic affirmations in *Becoming the Way We Are* and are used with the permission of the author.

Cover design: Terry Dugan
Illustrations: Jerry Smath

Library of Congress Cataloging-in-Publication Data

Help! for parents of children from ages three to six years.

(The Suggestion circle series; vol. 4)
Includes index.
1. Child rearing—United States. 2. Children—Care and hygiene—United States. I. Clarke, Jean Illsley. II. Parents for parents. III. Series.
HQ774.5.H45   1986   649'.123   86-18410
ISBN: 0-86683-454-0

87 88 89 90 OPM 10 9 8 7 6 5 4 3 2

Contents

CLUSTERS AND SUGGESTION CIRCLES

Appreciations

We offer our thanks to

- The parents at North City Cooperative Pre-school, who contributed many suggestions.
- The many other families who have contributed ideas for Suggestion Circles.
- Elizabeth, for her easygoing infancy and constant presence at our writing meetings.
- Nat Houtz, Gail Davenport, and Maggie Lawrence, for paving the way and making our job much easier.
- Liz Bentley, for her thoughtful insights and suggestions.
- Deane Gradous, for conceiving the idea of publishing Suggestion Circles in books.
- Pediatrician Christine Ternand, for writing **About Abuse** and for reading the Circles for medical accuracy.
- Our husbands and children, who encouraged us and who helped us find the space and time to write.
- All the facilitators of groups and classes, for running and saving Suggestion Circles for us.
- Nancy Nenovich, Mary Ann Lisk, Becky Monson, and Vivian Rouson-Gossett, for their dedication, support, humor, and word-processing skills.

—The Editors

Foreword

When I talk with groups of parents, they will often ask for advice: "What should I do when my child swears—or hits—or whines?" Parents often want "one right answer." Unfortunately, no one way is right for all people. Nothing works all the time.

The *HELP!* books are an exciting way to get new ideas for dealing with children. They offer several ideas for each concern, and your job as a parent is to decide what will work best for you and your child.

The task of the three- to six-year-old child is to find out about power and identity. This can be very disconcerting for parents, since children often investigate the use of power by challenging the routines and values as well as the people around them. As the child experiments, the guidance techniques that work one day may not work the next.

You can help children understand constructive power by letting them know you are looking for ways of handling conflict and by modeling good problem-solving skills. With the *HELP!* books, you have in your hands the ideas and experience of hundreds of parents and professionals.

The challenge of raising the three- to six-year-old is not how to force compliance, but how to use

your power so you both can win. The *HELP!*
books offer you many ways to do that.

—Elizabeth Crary,
Author of *Without Spanking or Spoiling, Kids
Can Cooperate*, and
the Problem-Solving Books:
I Want It, I Can't Wait, and
My Name Is Not Dummy

What Is This Book About?

This is a book written for parents by parents.

It is for the days when you don't know what to do or when what you're doing isn't working. It is *not* a theoretical book about the times when things are going smoothly. It *is* a book of specific, practical suggestions for handling different problems that parents have sought help for in parenting classes around the country.

These parents have participated in groups led by a facilitator who is trained in the techniques used in "Self-Esteem: A Family Affair" classes. One of these techniques, called the "Suggestion Circle," is used to collect options for parents with problems. Here's how it works. In class, members sit in a circle and listen to a parent describe a problem. Each member of the Circle then offers his or her best suggestion for dealing with it. In this way, the person with the problem benefits from the collective wisdom and experience of the whole group and goes home with a list of suggestions or options.

The Suggestion Circle process is different from brainstorming, which encourages people to offer every idea that comes to mind. It's also different from listening to the teacher or the expert provide "the correct answer." In a Suggestion Circle, *every* answer comes from an "authority," a parent, day-care provider, uncle, aunt, or grandparent. And every answer is "correct," since it worked for the person who discovered it—sometimes after many years of experience. The resulting list provides a variety of suggestions and encourages flexibility in the listener or reader. It may suggest a new way of perceiving the problem.

We chose these eighty Circles because they represent problems that we hear about repeatedly in classes or that seem particularly difficult for parents. Leaders collected the suggestions and asked the parents if we could share their responses with you in these books. Each Circle includes the name of the first facilitator who sent the problem to us and the location of the class or group. Since similar problems come up in different parts of the country, we have combined suggestions from more than one group.

You will notice that often the answers contradict one another. That needn't bother you. Parents and children and homes are different, and what works with one may not work with another or at another time.

You will find the Suggestion Circles grouped in clusters according to subject matter. We have eliminated any ideas that advocated violence, both because child abuse is illegal and because we do not believe violence helps children. We have also eliminated suggestions that implied that parents or children are helpless or that a problem was not serious. We assume that if parents ask for help, the problems are important and serious to them.

In the opening pages of the book, we have outlined the characteristic tasks of this stage of development and described how parents may abuse children if they misunderstand those tasks. We have also given short explanations of *affirmations*, *recycling*, and other topics that are important parts of the "Self-Esteem: A Family Affair" class and that are referred to in the Circles.

So here they are, some eighty Circles, eighty collections of the best ideas from parents who have been there, to you who are there now.

—The Editors

3

How to Use This Book

You can use this book to help you think. When you want ideas about how to solve a problem, look in the table of contents for a cluster title that seems to include your problem. For example, for eating problems, look under "Picky Eaters." Or look in the index for words that describe your problem (like *food* or *eating)* and read about the problems that sound most like yours.

Reading about what other parents have done will remind you that there are many ways to solve problems and that you can find and try out new ways that work for you and your child. If you read a list over several times, you will probably find ideas you missed the first time. Some of the suggestions may not fit your situation or your parenting style, and some of the lists contain contradictions, since there are lots of ways to raise children. Think about which suggestions sound useful for your particular problem.

Whenever you think of a suggestion that is not listed, write it in your book for future reference. *Our purpose is not to give "one right answer" but to support and stimulate your thinking by offering the wisdom of hundreds of the real child-rearing experts— parents themselves.*

Remember that these suggestions are *not* listed in an order of importance. They were offered by a circle of people. If we had printed them in circles, this would be a very big book! We offer them in lists to make a small and convenient book, not to imply that the top suggestion is best.

Use the short sections at the beginning and end of the book as you need them. For a picture of normal three- to six-year-old behavior, read **Ages and Stages** and **About Abuse**. You can use that information to think about whether your expectations are reasonable.

The **Affirmations for Growth** section is about healthy messages or beliefs that children this age need to decide are true for them. You can ponder these affirming messages and all the ways, verbal and nonverbal, in which you offer these ideas regularly to your children. The section called **Parents Get Another Chance—Recycling** reminds us that our own growth never stops and that we, too, are doing our own developmental tasks.

Look at **Time-Out**, **Preparing Your Child for Grade School**, or **Where to Go for Additional Support** for ways to help yourself. If you want to lead your own **Suggestion Circle**, see page 123.

So read and think. Honor yourself for the many things you do well with your children. Celebrate your growth and the growth of your children. Change when you need to. Remember that your parents did the best they could. You are doing the best you can. If you want to learn some new ways of parenting, it is never too late to start.

Note: In this book, we have alternated masculine and feminine pronouns; in one section or Circle, the child will be "she," in the next "he." In each case, please read "all children."

—Jean Illsley Clarke

Ages and Stages

What is preschool stage of development all about? You will find that the pretend play of three- to six-year-olds is charged with power themes as superheroes and monsters emerge. *Feeling powerful* is important to preschool children, and they can experience it in their *imagination* even if they often feel small and helpless in real life. Their *pretend play* is their way of trying on new roles and sorting out what's real from what's imaginary. Preschoolers seem to be quite clear about what is real and what is fantasy one minute and the next minute become terrified of a witch puppet or a ghost on TV.

Words help preschoolers to be important. The three-year-old asks, "Why?" The four-year-old says, "It's dumb and I hate it!" The five-year-old says, "How does it work?" They are learning that words have power; and sassing, whining, arguing, bad language, and baby talk all surface during this period.

Friends are very important to preschoolers, and they will play with imaginary friends if they can't play with real ones. Although social experiences are important, don't expect their social interactions to run smoothly. Preschoolers' play with others is usually quite bumpy, and during a morning of play you will probably observe tenderness, caring, imagination, laughter, shouts, screams, foul language, cooperation, arguing, and hitting and kicking, as children go about the business of getting to know each other. So keep social gatherings such as birthday parties simple and short. One hour long, and one guest for each year of age is a good rule if you want everyone to have a good time.

There is a new awareness of the sexes during the preschool period. Hospital play is a favorite game; it is children's way to understand their bodies. While parents will want to set limits on this play, they need not be upset about it. Around five, many boys refuse to use women's restrooms, causing inconvenience for their mothers. They have decided that there are two kinds of people in the world; male and female—and they are male. Signs or taunts of "No boys allowed" come from groups of girls, and boys often take a "boys only" attitude. Little boys may talk of marrying their mothers or sisters or girls they know. Girls do the same with fathers, brothers, and boys.

Two types of children may cause parents concern: the aggressive and the overly cautious. Aggressive children need large amounts of tolerance and open space. Contrary to the opinion of some, aggressive children are not necessarily hit by their parents or encouraged to hit others any more than nonaggressive children, but you do not take this type of child to a china shop. These are children who grasp life rather impulsively without a lot of forethought about the consequences. Constant limit-setting may not be effective with this type of child at this age. It is better to decide on a few important rules, such as not hurting others or damaging property and to temporarily ignore some things like making noise or clutter. These children respond in the long run to a lot of gentle guidance.

Overly cautious children, on the other hand, are watchers. They don't like to make mistakes. They need adults around who say with words and actions, "You don't have to hurry. Do this when you are ready." Pressuring them to perform before they are fully able does not work.

Young children go through four stages as they learn to defend their territory. The first stage is simply hitting or grabbing to get what they need. The second stage is the use of verbal aggression— words as power. Then bribery becomes an important tool: "If you give it to me you can come to my birthday party." Older preschoolers learn to collect allies. They learn how to gang up on another. These acts are not good or bad in themselves; they are just steps to higher levels of socialization. When you need to, set up some rules about these actions, but remember your child is handling the situations the best she can with limited experience. Handling things awkwardly is better for a child than not handling them at all.

Children ages three, four, and five break rules regularly and can be quite difficult to live with at times; but their rule-breaking is only the first step toward rule-keeping and rule-making, which will become an important developmental task during age six to twelve.

Because of frequent rule breaking, parents often wonder if they will have control of their preschoolers in an emergency. The answer is yes. Children know that their parents are smarter and stronger than they are, and that they will protect them from danger. In everyday matters, however, children will continue to balk at parental authority. It takes preschoolers a long time to teach their parents that they will no longer think the way parents say they should, that they are separate individual persons, and that they must be allowed to be themselves.

—Marilyn Grevstad

About Abuse

Child abuse and neglect are prevalent and perhaps epidemic in our society today. We feel strongly that all children are to be valued and cherished. We believe that children will be better protected when parents know the causes and signs of child abuse and when they learn ways to keep children safe.

Causes of Child Abuse

There are many causes of child abuse. Since this is not a book about the ills of society or emotionally disturbed individuals but about normal, healthy parents and children, we will address only the abuse that springs from parents' misunderstanding of normal growth and development of children at different ages. Sometimes, as children go about their developmental tasks, they do things that are misinterpreted by parents who may be overly severe or hurtful in an attempt to stop or control those normal behaviors.

The following behaviors of children this age are frequently misunderstood:

• Three- to six-year-old children are learning about their identity—including their sexual identity. This frequently leads to sexual play, including masturbation, "playing doctor," etc. If caring adults do not realize this is completely normal, they may overreact and physically or psychologically abuse children and give them a distorted view of their own sexuality. Parents should choose this time to explain to children that sexual organs will eventually be used to "make babies" and that sexual activity is a private activity, a source of pleasure, and a personal responsibility. It is my belief that by beginning to associate responsibility with sexuality at this stage, we as a society have the greatest hope of preventing teenage pregnancies.

- Also because these children are learning about sexuality, they may be practicing the flirtatious or coquettish behaviors they have seen adults model. Parents must be certain that all adults (and all babysitters) interacting with children know that sexually touching any child is completely wrong. It is also wrong to blame any child this age for "leading someone on." Adults are always responsible.

- Children this age are learning to recognize the difference between fantasy and reality. They often experiment with what is truth and what is a lie. It is important for caring adults to tell children what a lie is and to expect the truth. At the same time they should not overreact with physical or verbal abuse if children are lying.

- Children this age are very busy learning about and testing their own power. If parents find themselves in a power struggle, they may inappropriately use verbal or physical abuse to "win." When parents remember they are truly in charge, they can step out of the power struggle and be in charge. This way both parents and children win.

- Some children this age still need to learn toilet habits. Caring adults may forget that children are in charge of their own bodies, and in an effort to help them learn toilet habits, may become abusive. Both children and adults will benefit and have much happier lives if the adults acknowledge that children are in charge of their own bodies by allowing them to initiate their own toileting activities, despite the grandparents' or the neighbor's advice.
- Children this age are using rational thinking and show some early signs of adult behavior. Adults sometimes seize on this sign of new thinking as a signal to push children with a "hurry-and-grow-up-fast-to-take-care-of-me" message. It is important to let children be children.

Signs of Child Abuse

Since other adults or older children may abuse, here are some physical signs that may indicate abuse of a child this age:

- Circular bite marks, either adult- or child-size.
- Circular burns from cigarettes.
- Hand slap marks on buttocks or elsewhere.
- More than one bruise on the thighs or upper arms.
- Straight line bruises that may come from a belt or a ruler.
- Any hand marks.
- Unwillingness or overwillingness to display the genitalia, or inappropriate sexual or violent play with dolls.

- Any behavior problem, which may signal emotional or physical abuse.
- A child beginning to stutter after four years of age, or beginning to soil or wet after being trained.

Ways to Keep Children Safe

Children this age need careful structure for safety. Parents who do not abuse or neglect their children keep them safe by
- Refusing to leave a child alone in house or car.
- Always using car seats or safety belts when traveling with a child in the car.
- Setting clear and firm limits for babysitters by discussing and leaving of list of do's and don'ts.
- Monitoring outside play and water safety.
- Making certain that other adults understand what the children need.
- Listening carefully if children report anything that would suggest abusive behavior from other adults.
- Teaching children accurate terms for all body parts, including penis, testicles, vagina, vulva, and breasts.
- Teaching children safety skills, like saying no and respecting their own and others' bodies.

If you suspect abuse of any kind, find a way to protect the child. Get help if you need it. Report the abuser to the child protection service in your area. See **Where to Go for Additional Help**.

—Christine Ternand, M.D.

Affirmations for Growth

At each period or stage of growth in children's lives there are certain tasks they need to master and certain decisions they need to make if they are to grow into loving, capable, responsible adults.

Parents can help children master these tasks by providing safe, structured, stimulating environments and experiences. Parents can encourage their children to make appropriate decisions by giving their children affirmations.

What are affirmations? Affirmations are all the things we do or say that imply that children are lovable and capable. We affirm children with our words and our actions, our body language, our facial expressions, and our tone of voice.

Here are some special affirming messages that will help children during this stage of growth. At this age, children are exploring their identity and ways of being powerful, acquiring lots of information, starting to learn socially appropriate behavior, developing their imagination, and trying out different ways of relating to other people.

Affirmations for Identity and Power

• You can explore who you are and find out who other people are.
• You can be powerful and ask for help at the same time.

- You can try out different roles and ways of being powerful.
- You can find out the results of your behavior.
- All of your feelings are OK with me.
- You can learn what is pretend and what is real.
- I love who you are.

You *give* these affirmations by the way you interact with the child, encourage his or her imagination, supply information to endless questions, expect cause- and-effect thinking, reward socially appropriate behavior, and enforce limits. You can also *say* these affirmations directly in a supportive, loving way.

Of course, you have to believe the affirmations yourself, or they become confusing or crazy double messages. If you don't understand or believe an affirmation, don't give that one until you do believe it. If we tell children something we don't believe, they see our body language, respond to our tone of voice, and get a conflicting message. In order for your children to believe these affirmations, it must be truly important to you for them to build identity, claim power, and move toward autonomy, toward being independent and responsible for themselves. Before children can learn to respond to others in an independent, honoring way, they must establish their own identity, their sense of "this is who I am."

Since we never outgrow the need for these health-giving messages, children at this age continue to need messages from the three earlier stages. The affirmations for Being are about our right to exist and have needs.

Affirmations for Being

- I'm glad you are alive.
- You belong here.
- What you need is important to me.
- I'm glad you are you.
- You can grow at your own pace.
- You can feel all of your feelings.
- I love you, and I care for you willingly.

The affirmations for Doing focus on our need to reach out and explore.

Affirmations for Doing

- You can explore and experiment, and I will support and protect you.
- You can use all of your senses when you explore.
- You can do things as many times as you need to.
- You can know what you know.
- You can be interested in everything.
- I like to watch you initiate and grow and learn.
- I love you when you are active and when you are quiet.

The affirmations for Thinking support thinking and independence.

Affirmations for Thinking

- I'm glad you are starting to think for yourself.
- It's OK for you to be angry, and I won't let you hurt yourself or others.
- You can say no and push and test limits as much as you need to.

- You can learn to think for yourself, and I will think for myself.
- You can think and feel at the same time.
- You can know what you need and ask for help.
- You can become separate from me, and I will continue to love you.

Children who decided not to believe all these messages at a younger age have another chance to incorporate them now. Remember, it is never too late for you to start giving these affirmations.

You can read more about what affirmations mean and don't mean and how to use them in families in Clarke's *Self-Esteem: A Family Affair*. These affirmations are adapted from Pamela Levin's *Becoming the Way We Are*. (See **Resources**.)

When you discover additional affirmations that your child needs, write them in your book and give them to your child.

—Jean Illsley Clarke

Parents Get Another Chance— Recycling

Parents often delight in young children who are trying on identity roles and learning new social skills and developing imagination by making up wonderful and strange things and asking a thousand questions. But sometimes those parents feel tired. They run out of answers and patience and wonder who they are and how they got this demanding job.

One of the benefits of this period of children's growth for parents is that they can recreate a new sense of autonomy. They can rework or recycle their own concept of self-identity and the ways they use their power, their creativity, and their imagination.

What Is Recycling?

Recycling is the name given to the rhythmic, cyclical growth process that individuals go through, often without noticing it, in which they learn to do important developmental tasks in ever more competent and sophisticated ways. Pamela Levin discusses this theory in *Becoming the Way We Are*. Recycling does not mean that we adults regress to a childlike state, but rather that our life experiences demand that we continually develop more skillful ways of doing life-supporting tasks. Besides having a natural rhythm of our own, we as parents are often triggered to recycle whatever stages our children are in. I have talked with hundreds of parents about this idea. Many of them have reported, often with some surprise, that they *are* working on some of the same tasks as their children. It is a normal, healthy, and hopeful aspect of living with growing children.

Recycling the Tasks of Becoming Separate and Thinking

Parents of children who are busy discovering who they are and how to do things can use this period not only to support their children's growth but also to update their own identity and use of power. They can ask anew the question, "Who am I?" and "What about my relationships with all those other people?" and "Do I want to change the ways I relate?"

This is a good opportunity for parents to think about power. "Do I think power is good or bad in itself or only the way in which people use it?" "Am I denying that I have the power to improve my life?" "Do I like the way I use my power?" "Do I whine instead of asking in a straightforward way for what I need?" "Would I and my family be better off if I bullied less? manipulated less? shared power more?"

The affirmations that are helpful to our children are also healthy for us. (See page 14.) Because many of us never received or decided not to believe some of those healthy messages (or only believe them partly), this is an ideal time to accept those messages for ourselves and to claim more of our ability to be whole, healthy, joyful adults. If you didn't get the affirmations you needed first time around, you can take them now as you offer them to your children.

—Jean Illsley Clarke

A. The Identity of the Preschooler

My four-year-old creates wonderful stories, but he creates them when I need an answer to a question. How can I encourage that creativity and yet have him give me the answer I need?

- Be clear with him when you need an answer. Avoid the words "truth" and "lying." Say, "You make up wonderful stories, but right now I need the answer to my question."
- Use body language (a wink) or words to indicate you know when he is telling a story.
- Spend time telling stories *with* him.
- Ask, "Is that pretend or real?"
- Read him the story about the boy who cried wolf and discuss it.
- This is typical behavior for four-year-olds. Read the chapter in Clarke's *Self-Esteem: A Family Affair* about three- to six-year-olds. (See **Resources**.)
- As a family, take turns telling the same story or adding on to one that someone starts.
- When you answer his questions make sure that you are direct with your answer. This will show him how to answer directly.
- Support his creativity by helping him record his stories on a tape recorder or have him dictate them for you to write down.
- Ask your question and allow lots of time for the story.
- At other times ask some questions in a way that he can make a choice; and honor his choice.

Thanks to Sue Hansen, Circle from Bellevue, Washington

My child was frightened when she saw a scary ghost on TV and said, "It won't come out of the TV, will it, Mommy?"

- Say, "No it won't."
- Turn off the TV and talk about it.
- Say, "You're right, it won't come out of the TV. Some things are pretend, aren't they?"
- Say, "What you saw on TV was either made by people using machines or a person covered up by a sheet."
- Borrow or rent a VCR and camera and let your child see herself on screen.
- Let her play ghost with a sheet if she wishes.
- Say, "When you see scary things in books or TV, you can come and ask me about them."
- Tell your child about pretend things that scared you when you were little.
- Tell her "No, it's pretend just like when you play dress-up or space woman."
- It's normal for kids this age to be confused about what's real and what isn't. So hang in there and be ready to answer a lot of this kind of question.

Thanks to Carole Gesme, Circle from Wayzata, Minnesota

How much time is OK for a four-year-old to spend watching TV?

• Watch TV about as often as you go out to a movie. Turn it on only as a special activity to do with your family.

• Screen the content beforehand. Know why you are turning the TV on.

• Read *The Read-Aloud Handbook* by Jim Trelease. It tells parents how to help kids do less TV and more reading. (See **Resources**.)

• None.

• Read *The Berenstain Bears and Too Much TV* by the Berenstains to your child. (See **Resources**.)

• Select two quality shows your child is allowed regularly (*Sesame Street*, cartoons, *Mister Rogers*).

• Read Marie Winn's *The Plug-In Drug* and decide what your TV criteria are. (See **Resources**.)

• Decide how much TV you enjoy watching with your child, and that should be the determining amount.

• Dramatizations and cartoons should be monitored before age seven. Preschoolers are still working on separating fantasy from reality.

• You are in charge of the TV for your child. It is not in charge of you.

(See also A-2.)

Thanks to Mary Paananen, Circle from Seattle, Washington

My four-and-a-half-year-old thinks our divorce is her fault. What should I say?

- Say, "No, the divorce is not your fault. Mom and Dad have different ideas about how to live, and since we cannot agree on these we choose to live apart."
- Tell your child, "When Dad and I married, we thought we would be together all of your life. Now we don't want to be together. We both love you and our love for you won't change."
- Say, "You might feel that our divorce was caused by you or things you have done. It was not."
- Encourage your child to talk about what she believes she did wrong to cause the divorce. Listen to her and reassure her that nobody is good all the time and that children do not cause divorces.
- Say, "Divorces are between big people. Little people do not cause them."
- Touch her often and hold her close.
- Say, "My love for your father is one thing. A mother's love for her child is different. I can stop loving your father and keep on loving you."
- Give her the affirmation "You can learn what is pretend and what is real. What is real is that adults decide about divorce. Kids do not." (See page 14.)

Thanks to Ellen Peterson, Circle from Lafayette, California

What do I say to my three-year-old when he asks, "Where is Daddy?" He died when my son was eight months.

- Talk with him as often as he needs about his dad.
- Make sure you don't give more information than your child is asking for.
- Create a special book for him about his dad with pictures and any other reminders that he may keep with him and look at whenever he wants.
- Tell him what you believe about what happens to people when they die.
- Tell him the same story of what you believe over and over again, and add to it as he gets older and understands more.
- Read *The Dead Bird* by Margaret Brown, a simple and beautifully written story about some children's experience upon finding a dead bird in the woods. (See **Resources**.)
- Cry with him!
- *Life Is Goodbye—Life Is Hello* by Alla Bozarth-Campbell is a book for adults about grieving. You may find it helpful to you and him. (See **Resources**.)
- My father died when I was three, and I wish my mother had talked about him—the little things he liked, his ideas, and what he hoped for me.
- Say, "I loved your Dad. I love you, too."

Thanks to Mary Paananen, Circle from Seattle, Washington

My daughter is shy and dreads show-and-tell at school. What do I do?

- Role-play the situation with her.
- Point out the things she does well.
- Send a note to the teacher asking for ideas on how to cope with the shyness.
- Invite classmates home to play.
- Read *The Shy Child* by Zimbardo and Radl. (See **Resources**.)
- Shy feelings are normal for kids this age. Unless it seems really extreme, accept her for doing and feeling what she needs to right now.
- Have puppet shows and plays with the family.
- Suggest she wear her most comfortable or special clothing.
- Sit down together and brainstorm. Listen to her solutions.
- Tell about times when you feel shy and what things you do, like going with a friend or watching until you feel comfortable.
- Suggest she skip it for a few weeks.
- Don't feel obligated to solve the problem for her.
- Give her the Being affirmations. (See page 16.)

Thanks to Nat Houtz, Circle from Seattle, Washington

How can I teach my five-year-old not to be greedy? What can I say to my child who has been given a gift and thirty seconds later asks for something else new?

- Say, "OK, the toy you want costs five dollars. I'll help you figure out how you can earn the money."
- Say, "No."
- "I hear you, and I can't afford another one right now."
- "OK! Now I know what to get for your birthday."
- Ask him to think of something he wants that doesn't cost anything.
- Have a wish-list on the refrigerator to keep track of special wants, and honor those wants on appropriate occasions.
- Maybe he is trying to keep up with his friends. Be sure you and he take time for noncompetitive games. See *The New Games* book by Andrew Fluegelman. (See **Resources**.)
- Help your child appreciate his new toy. Ask him to tell you all the things he likes about it.

(See also F-6.)

Thanks to Mary Paananen, Circle from Seattle, Washington

How do you teach kids to think about feelings?

- Plan to share at dinner or family time one *feeling* about something you did during the day.
- Notice what they already know about feelings. Compliment them on that.
- Read books about feelings such as Ancona's *I Feel: A Picture Book of Emotions*. (See **Resources**.)
- Give words to use: grumpy, tired, sad, joyful, lonely, or excited.
- Ask, "Where in your body do you feel that?"
- Practice saying with your children statements that tell the difference between I think...and I feel....
- Make a "feeling wheel" for each member of the family with a dial to point to how he or she is feeling from time to time.
- Talk with your children about their feelings and how they think others are feeling when certain things happen.
- Play this game: One person says the feeling word and the other responds by making the face that expresses that feeling.
- Let your child know that all feelings are OK to have.
- Tell stories about how you felt and what you did when you were small.
- Read the chapter about three- to six-year-olds in Clarke's *Self-Esteem: A Family Affair*. (See **Resources**.)

Thanks to Elizabeth Crary, Circle from Seattle, Washington

How can I help my four-year-old daughter learn to solve problems?

• Kids this age solve lots of problems every day (what clothes to wear, what to play next, etc.). Catch your daughter doing this well and remind her of this when she begins solving her next problem.

• Sometimes problems need to be divided into pieces. Show her how to do this.

• Tell her that problem-solving takes practice like skating and bike riding. Assure her that you love her and will be there if she needs to check things out.

• Read Betsy Crary's series of books on solving problems. (See **Resources**.)

• Play the game that poses problems for kids: "What would you do if a raccoon walked into the kitchen right now?" "What are three ways to get to the park?"

• Talk out loud as you problem-solve so she can hear you work through problems.

• If she likes to draw, ask her to draw the problem and all possible solutions on paper.

• Walk through the situation yourself, using familiar objects to practice. This will let her see choices might be possible or not possible.

• Don't rush in and solve all her problems. Wait and say, "You can solve this problem. I will help you think of ways, if you need me."

Thanks to Mary Paananen, Circle from Seattle, Washington

B. Behavior Problems

My son talks all day. How can I get him to stop when I need to do something else? We have new twins.

• Give him a tape recorder to play with.
• Let him know he can play with a toy now and talk about it later.
• Tell him you will have special time just for him. Set the timer so you remember, and then let him chatter on and on, while you listen attentively.
• Let him sit on your lap for five minutes for attention, while you do what you are doing.
• Clearly tell him what he is going to do next. Prepare him as much as you can.
• Show him a talking place—a chair with a bear to talk to, or a box, or someplace where he can go tell his story, if he has a burning desire to do so.
• Say, "This is my time to talk. You may stay close by." Stick to it.
• Realize that this will pass. Kids this age need to ask a lot of questions. Include him in conversation whenever you can.
• Sometimes give your child total attention. Other times say, "I'm doing something else now, but I can partly listen to you."
• You are responsible for teaching him when to talk and when not to. He is responsible for his feelings. Encourage him not to feel hurt when you stop him from talking.

Thanks to Sue Hansen, Circle from Bellevue, Washington

My five-year-old colors on the walls. She does it secretly, while I am caring for the baby. What can I do?

• The issue may not be the coloring but her way of acting out about something else. Ask her to talk about her feelings about the new baby. Accept her feelings and suggest ways she can deal with them.

• Set up a coloring mural on one wall in the house. Show it to people and brag about her coloring on it.

• Control the crayons. She can earn the right to use them again by using them properly.

• Expect the child to help clean the wall.

• Get a sitter for the baby, and you and your daughter have an afternoon doing what she wants to do.

• Be sure to spend fifteen to twenty minutes every day with her in one-to-one time doing what she chooses to do, not what you think would be good for her.

• Tell her stories about when she was her little sister's age and how you cared for her.

• Offer to rock her and hold her.

• Tell her she does not need to do this to get your attention; then make sure you have periods of time alone with her.

• Put the crayons out of reach. Tell her they are to be used at the table only. Enforce that rule.

• Give her lots of love and the Being affirmations. (See page 16.)

Thanks to Carol Gesme, Circle from Anoka, Minnesota

How can I handle my four-and-a-half-year-old's terrible behavior? He seems to try to get me mad. He is worse every day, and I just don't understand because the baby is so easygoing.

- Give him lots of private time with you, and give lots and lots of positive attention.
- Let him know he can ask for special time with you. Give it as soon as you can.
- Say, "You don't need to do that to get my attention." Then be willing to pay attention when he asks for it.
- Make sure you don't start thinking of "our good child" and "our bad child." Honor the positive as well as the negative in both.
- Double up on affirmations for Being. Read Clarke's *Self-Esteem: A Family Affair*. (See **Resources**.)
- Give him lots of physical touch—carrying, rocking, and massages.
- Give more three- to six-year-old affirmations for power. (See page 14.)
- Read him *TA for Tots* by Alvyn Freed. (See **Resources**.)
- Talk to him about the things that have happened as a result of the baby's arrival. Also say, "Gee, the baby takes a lot of time right now, doesn't he?"
- Tell him it is all right to feel angry or jealous and that he is to use words to tell you his feelings.

Thanks to Susie Montgomery, Circle from Walnut Creek, California

My child whines about everything, but especially when asked to play alone. What can I do?

- Give her lots of your attention at times when she is not whining or wanting something.
- Read *Your Three-Year-Old* by Ames and Ilg. (See **Resources**.)
- Have others compliment her for using words. You do this too. Give her no response for whining.
- Tell her to use words instead of whining. When she does, give her a hug or a sticker.
- Like a broken record, tell her each time she whines, "I don't talk to whining girls," and then don't talk to her.
- Have a family conference and ask others how they feel about the whining. Make sure no one gives her attention for it until she stops the behavior.
- Set aside special time for her.
- Explain that you will not tolerate this. Use a chart and stars and then a trip to the zoo as a reward for improved behavior.
- Explain to her that everybody spends some time alone. Use a timer and start with fifteen minutes of play.
- Tell her, "I like it when you ask for what you want in your normal voice."
- Show her what you want by using a pleasant voice and then ask her to do the same.

Thanks to Marilyn Grevstad, Circle from Seattle, Washington

My children, ages four and three, fight in the back seat of the car while I am driving until I am terribly distracted. How can I get them to stop?

• Stop the car at the first safe place. Say, "When you are ready to follow our rules about being quiet in the car, I will go on." This works best if they are going someplace interesting.
• If what the kids are doing is not dangerous, ignore them. Sing "The Wheels on the Bus Go Round and Round" or "Old MacDonald."
• Stop the car. Tell them you feel frustrated and distracted when they behave that way and that you cannot safely drive the car until they stop.
• At the end of the drive give stickers for good behavior. Tell them beforehand.
• Put one child in the front seat and one in the back. We make a chart by weeks for who gets to sit in the front seat.
• Play tapes they will enjoy while traveling. "Sesame Street" tapes are good for this age.
• Have a car-pack of toys they can use only while in the car.
• Play a "Can you see . . . ?" game.

Thanks to Deane Gradous, Circle from St. Paul, Minnesota

What do I do about insulting back talk from my three-year-old child?

- Ignore it. It may take a while, but eventually she won't find it interesting.
- Discipline her for it. Remove a privilege for an hour.
- Tell her people who back talk sometimes end up without anyone to play with.
- Talk to her. Help her understand your feelings.
- Use time-out. (See page 114.)
- Tell her, "Say words I like to hear like, 'Mommy, you're adorable' or 'Mommy, you're courageous.'" Then fall on your knees and say thank you. Drama is sometimes effective.
- Show her how you want her to express her feelings without using back talk.
- Have a "play" back-talk time when she sits on a stool and talks back for five minutes.
- Tell her she is a kind person and that you will be glad when she has finished trying out back talk.
- Listen to find out whether others in the family talk back and get by with it. If they do, change that and back off of your three-year-old.

(See also B-7.)

Thanks to Marilyn Grevstad, Circle from Seattle, Washington

How do I solve the problem of my three-year-old calling people "stupid idiot" in the grocery store?

- Listen to yourself and other family members. If any of the other family members use "stupid idiot" have them stop. Let the three-year-old see how the older person is learning to stop.
- Say, "You're important to me. It is hard for me to hear those words. I expect you to say, 'Hello' instead."
- Tell him he doesn't have to like everyone, but he does have to be polite.
- Make a face at him to signal him to stop, then rub noses.
- Ignore it. You speak pleasantly to people so he will learn how.
- Play with words. "Stupid, drupid, nupid, idiot, midiot, gidiot." Turn it into a silly game.
- Say, "I'm surprised. I don't expect you to say mean things, and I am really sorry to hear this."
- Tell him that people like to be spoken to respectfully.
- Give him lots of positive response when he does communicate well.
- Help him find "angry" words that are acceptable in your family.

Thanks to Roxy Chuchna, Circle from Albert Lea, Minnesota

My five-year-old has picked up some "dirty" words and hand signals from a friend who has an older brother. She has been using them around home.

- Ignore it.
- Say, "If you'd like to use bathroom talk, please go into the bathroom and close the door. I don't want to hear it."
- Use a star chart to mark the days she goes without using the words or hand signals.
- Show her some finger play games to use instead.
- Say, "That is inappropriate for a child your age. Please don't use it."
- Tell her to try them out in her room but not in front of other people.
- Say that it is not appropriate for her. If her friend uses it, tell the friend she is not to do that when she is with you.
- Catch her when she hasn't done it and reward her for not doing it.
- Better to ignore it completely.
- Teach her some new words to say instead.
- Explain to her that many people regard the use of these words and motions as insulting and that you are glad to talk with her about them so she won't use them.

Thanks to Sue Hansen, Circle from Bellevue, Washington

My four-year-old lies. How do I get him to stop?

- Explain why you don't want him to lie.
- Show him that you appreciate him when he tells the truth.
- Ignore the lies. He will watch you telling the truth and learn how to do that.
- When he says something that is not true, tell him you don't believe him.
- Give him a consequence for lying. Take away a privilege.
- Tell him you will be glad when he stops lying and that you expect him to do that soon.
- State that you know it is a lie and that he makes up good stories.
- Give him a hug when he tells the truth.
- Think about why he is lying. Is it to avoid discipline? If so, is the discipline too severe?
- Spend time making up a story together. Make sure that he understands that this is different from something that really happened.
- Ask him if it is pretend or real.
- Teach him the difference between a lie and a mistake made from having inaccurate information.

(See also A-1.)

Thanks to Suzanne Morgan, Circle from Albert Lea, Minnesota

When I tell my three-year-old to do something she either says "no" or just doesn't do the task. What can I do?

- Get her attention by being close to her when you give the command.
- Use time-out. (See page 114.)
- Use eye level communication.
- Let her know that you love her whether she says yes or no.
- Ignore bad behavior and emphasize good behavior.
- Give only one direction at a time.
- Don't hurry her.
- Ask her nicely. If you get no response, pick her up firmly and put her where you want her to be.
- Look at what you are asking her to do to be sure it is suitable for a three-year-old. (See **Ages and Stages**.)
- Repeat the command so that it conveys the fact that there are no choices.
- Ask her to make a choice between two things you are willing for her to do.
- Be sure you are "telling" her. Don't "ask" unless no is an OK answer.

Thanks to Margie Black, Circle from Eden Prairie, Minnesota

What do I do when my three-year-old has a temper tantrum and goes out of control when told "no"?

• Sit with him in a rocking chair, hold him tight but don't hurt him and say, "I'm not going to let go of you until you calm down."

• Sit on the floor with your back against the wall. Wrap your arms and legs around the child and say, "I'll hold you until you calm down."

• Kneel in front of him and say, "I am not afraid of your anger. I will not let you hurt yourself or anyone else."

• Take him by the shoulders, look him straight in the eye, and say, "I'm sorry but I won't allow you to act that way. That is unacceptable behavior in this house."

• Put him in a time-out corner. (See page 114.)

• Give him Being affirmations. At a calm time make statements about grown-ups being in charge of this household. (See page 16.)

• Watch and observe if this is happening at a particular time of day. If so, find some special activities for him to do at this time. Taking a bath can be relaxing.

Thanks to Jean Clarke, Circle from Wayzata, Minnesota

How do I keep my children with me while I'm shopping?

- Use a backpack or Snugli for one and hold on to the other's hand.
- Allow plenty of time.
- Have them stay in or push a stroller.
- Tie a balloon to each one's wrist and ask them to keep the balloon near you.
- Do not go when the children are tired, hungry, or anxious.
- Trade babysitting with a friend so you can go alone sometimes.
- Keep shopping trips short.
- Discuss plans and expectations in advance.
- Take a toy along for each to carry.
- For staying with you, give them a box of animal crackers. If they don't stay, put the crackers back on the shelf.
- Put a sticker on each child's hand to remind them to stay close to you.
- Role-play before the trip. Practice good "shopping manners." Give rewards afterwards.

Thanks to Mary Ellen O'Keefe, Circle from Bellevue, Washington

My three-year-old hits and shoves other children.

- When it happens, pick him up and take him to his room. Don't say "Next time" or other idle threats.
- Use time-out. (See page 114.)
- Say, "Be gentle."
- Ask him to watch how other children play and try ways besides hitting and shoving.
- Tell him to use words when he is angry and reward him when he does.
- Give him a big pillow to hit and shove.
- Show him specific ways to relate to another child. "Give Nicky the toy or jump with Danny."
- Give him extra loving at other times.
- Look him in the eye and say, "You are capable. You can find other ways to play."
- Tell him, "That doesn't work because other children learn to do it back."

Thanks to Marilyn Grevstad, Circle from Seattle, Washington

I need help dealing with a three-year-old girl who continually bites.

- Give her time-out periods! Four minutes or less. (See page 114.)
- Have her bite a lemon, lime, or apple.
- Tell her she has to stop. Mean it. Don't smile or brag about how much she bites.
- Explain that this behavior is not appropriate. Ask her what she will do to help the person she has bitten to feel better.
- Consistently explain that biting hurts people, and we do not hurt other people. Keep with it. Don't hurt her.
- Give her lots of hugging. Tell her to ask for hugs instead of biting.
- Have her choose a toy or pillow to bite.
- Ask, "Would you like to be bitten?"
- If she starts to bite you, stop her immediately: Hold her tight (don't hurt her) while you say, "No biting!"
- Give her clear I-messages about how you feel when she bites you.
- Tell her "I love you, and I will not let you hurt me or other people."
- Teach her to kiss instead.
- Evaluate her schedule and notice when she bites. Make changes to prevent opportunities for biting if possible.

Thanks to Carole Gesme, Circle from Anoka, Minnesota

How can we get our child to mind without hitting her? She is stubborn.

- Stop hitting and tell her you are stopping and that she will be minding words and looks from now on.
- When you tell her to do something, look her directly in the eye and say, "I expect ." Have clear, definite expectations!
- Try giving your child more specific information about what you want her to do.
- Allow her to do things her own way whenever possible.
- Honor when her no is appropriate.
- Do not give a choice when there is no choice. When there is a choice say, "Do you want to . . . ?" And honor her no if she says no.
- Explain reason and expectation and consequence.
- Define your family as a team and tell her about her part.
- Teach her about times when it is important to be "stubborn" or tenacious.
- Look in her eyes at a quiet time and say, "I love you. I want to spend time having fun together. I'm not going to hit any more."

Thanks to Mary Paananen, Circle from Seattle, Washington

C. Brothers, Sisters, and Other Kids

I feel like a judge. I have a four-year-old and seven-year-old. When I haven't seen the incident, how can I evaluate it when one comes to me and says she's been hurt?

- Listen to each separately.
- Tell them you will help each child file a written complaint for you to consider. Write down what they dictate. Giving attention to each usually diffuses the anger.
- Read the book *Raising Brothers and Sisters Without Raising the Roof* by the Calladines. (See **Resources**.)
- You can't.
- Read Ames's and Haber's *He Hit Me First*. It is about sibling rivalry and helped me know I didn't have to be the referee at certain ages. (See **Resources**.)
- Explain that you did not see the incident so you cannot judge.
- Check to see if she is hurt and care for her. Don't talk about the other child.
- Ask "What do you want me to do?" Be clear and definite about what you will and will not do.
- Listen to her report without evaluating. Say, "Thanks for letting me know how this incident looks to you."
- Don't try to be fair because you can't; children will expect it if you try.

(See also B-3, B-13, C-3)

Thanks to Joanie Mack, Circle from Everett, Washington

How should I answer my child when he asks, "Do you love me or my sister the best?"

- Take your son on your lap and say, "I love you both very much. I don't think about loving one of you the best." Then look inside yourself to be sure that is true.
- "You are my favorite four-year-old son and no one can take your place. I love you."
- Give him all the Being affirmations. (See page 16.)
- Don't say, "I love you both the same," because each love affair is different.
- Hug him, rumple or tickle him a little, and say, "I have plenty of love for you both!"
- Say, "I don't love anyone 'the best.' Here is what I love about you. I love you because you are my son, I love the way you. . . ."
- Say, "I have a huge barrel full of love for each of you, and lots more empty barrels for when those run over."
- Say, "I love you both. You do some things better and she does some things better and that has nothing to do with my love."
- Say, "That question does not have an answer. Do you want me to read you a story?"

Thanks to Gail Nordeman, Circle from Cincinnati, Ohio

How can I handle teasing between my children?

- Find something that the two who are teasing can work on together as partners in a cooperative activity, like building a tent.
- Listen. If you decide the teasing is a way of having some fun or to establish position, allow it. Stop teasing that's vicious.
- Separate them.
- Read *Kids Can Cooperate* by Elizabeth Crary. (See **Resources**.)
- Establish rules about teasing for the whole family.
- Don't be a referee.
- Give your children words they may use when they are teased such as, "No one in my family is stupid."
- If their behavior is destructive, intervene.
- Read them the *Warm Fuzzie Tale* by Claude Steiner and ask them to give each other warm fuzzies. (See **Resources**.)
- Remove yourself so they don't have an audience.
- Be sure you don't tease them.
- Young children can take time out to think. Help each of your children identify the feelings they are having.
- It's OK to stop the teasing when you've had it. Take care of yourself.

Thanks to Gail Davenport, Circle from Lynnwood, Washington

My three-and-a-half-year-old boy picks on his eighteen-month-old sister. What am I doing wrong?

- Don't waste time feeling guilty. Show him what you want him to do instead.
- Nothing, unless one of them is getting hurt. Give your son extra loving and Being messages. (See page 16.)
- Are you expecting yourself to be a "perfect mom with perfect kids"? If so, stop. It is too great a burden on the kids. Get help if you need it.
- Get time for yourself. These exploring years are demanding on the parent.
- Your daughter may be bugging her brother for attention. It takes two to tango.
- Your son is just learning how to play with others. Up until this point most of his play has been parallel play. You can't expect them to be wonderful playmates at this age.
- Ask each of them, "What do you want from me?" and trust them to establish a relationship that is right for them.
- Make a place for your son's things where your daughter can't get into them.

(See also B-13, B-16.)

Thanks to Marilyn Grevstad, Circle from Seattle, Washington

What do I do when my children threaten or hit each other and me?

- You are responsible for a safe environment. You decide when to step in and when to keep out.
- Make sure that you and other adults are not using threats around them.
- Interrupt and offer a toy from your emergency toy box or a snack or a walk.
- Help your kids make a list of things to do instead of hitting.
- Tell them, "It's OK to be angry but not OK to hit."
- For threats to you: Pick up the one who is threatening, give hugs and kisses, and say, "Threats don't work with me. Ask for what you want."
- Say, "Stop your threats. This is not television. Work it out."
- Don't listen to the threats. Don't respond positively or negatively.
- Close your eyes and visualize your children having fun together.
- Acknowledge their anger and help them find safe ways to express it. Hold a pillow for them to hit, provide a *big* piece of paper with bright paint for painting, or let them hit a stool with a ruler.
- Don't blame yourself. Children this age are testing their physical and verbal power.

Thanks to Samara Kemp, Circle from Modesto, California

Our four-year-old doesn't like anyone except one child in preschool. What do I say when he says to other kids, "I don't like you"?

- Explain it is OK to feel that way and he can keep it to himself or tell you.
- Ignore it. This may have more to do with words than feelings.
- Say, "I like you" to the kid he rejected and "I like you, too" to your son.
- Don't say, "You don't really mean that" because he may.
- I know how you feel. It sounds awful when your child says, "I don't like you." Remind yourself that he is testing out his own power and this is a developmental stage.
- Tell him he's important and you love him. Let him have the consequences from other children and help him see his part in it.
- Ask the teacher for suggestions. She knows the kids.
- Remember when you were this age? I loved someone one minute and hated them the next.
- Don't say, "Tell him you're sorry you said that," because if he isn't, it teaches him to be dishonest about his feelings.

Thanks to Maggie Lawrence, Circle from Edmonds, Washington

My five-year-old's best friend doesn't like her any more. How can I help her?

- Give her lots of hugs.
- Listen to her.
- Don't try to make the hurt go away. It hurts to lose a friend. She will learn to handle it.
- Honor her feelings and yours. You may want your child's life to always be smooth, but it can't be.
- Make her some lemonade. Invite some kids over, if she wishes.
- Tell her you love her.
- Don't hurry her. Let her take time to get over this.
- Draw the outline of her body on butcher paper and have the family write things they like about her, inside the outline.
- Don't make it worse than it is. The friend may be back tomorrow.

Thanks to Deane Gradous, Circle from Wayzata, Minnesota

D. Not Again! Toddlerhood Revisited

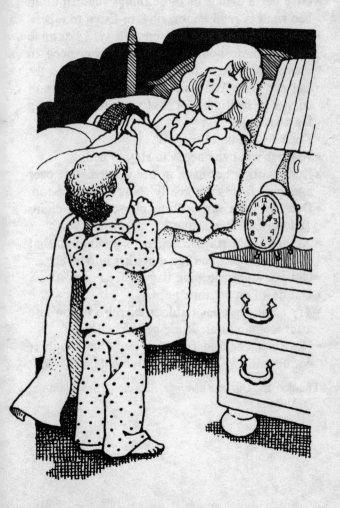

How can I keep my three-year-old daughter in bed at bedtime?

- Give her a choice of three things she can do in bed such as read books, sing, or listen to tapes.
- Perhaps she is not tired enough yet. Examine your bedtime hour and decide if you need to make it half an hour later.
- Let her know you love her and that you are in charge of bedtime, not that you are gearing up for a struggle.
- Keep a light on in the hall.
- Ask her what she needs to stay in bed.
- Keep putting her back in bed immediately over and over, firmly but gently. No talk and no fun.
- Don't spring a new bedtime plan on her at night. Tell her in the morning.
- As long as she stays in her room, don't insist that she stay in bed. You can move her into bed later.
- Get her a new sleeping bag to sleep in.
- Cut down on daytime naps.
- Try some vigorous outdoor exercise in the late afternoon and quiet time before bed.
- Have her checked for allergies. Our daughter got up until we took out the feathers and wool.

Thanks to Darlene Montz, Circle from Yakima, Washington

My three-year-old child gets up during the night and interrupts our sleep.

- Pick him up, no words, no payoff, no anger, and put him back in bed.
- Let him sleep with you or in your room in a sleeping bag.
- During the day ask him what might help him get himself back to sleep: teddy bear, music, etc., and make a plan with him.
- Tell him when he *can* come to your bed, in the morning, for example.
- Give him time to talk about nightmares and fears.
- Tell him what you expect: "You will stay in bed and if you wake, you will turn over and go back to sleep."
- Let the child turn on the light and look at books by himself during the night, but make it clear he cannot come to your room.
- Have the less angry parent deal with it. Your anger reinforces his behavior.
- Have the more annoyed parent deal with it. He or she will be firmer and end it sooner.
- Take him back to bed and lie down with him for a few minutes.

Thanks to Ellen Peterson, Circle from Walnut Creek, California

My three-year-old is wetting her pants again. She was trained before the baby came. What can I do?

- We've been that route. Put her in diapers for now. For my child it only lasted two weeks.
- Carry a change of clothes.
- Remind her to go to the bathroom, or take her every so often.
- Give her a treat when she goes to the bathroom or stays dry.
- Continue to use rubber sheets.
- Be sure she has alone time with you without the baby along.
- Let it be. It's a trauma for the child to have a new family member.
- Tell the child she can feel when she has to go to the bathroom and she can ask you to go with her. There is plenty of time to go.
- Ask if she wants diapers again. If so, let her wear them.
- Give her lots of love and Being affirmations. (See page 16.)
- Put up a sign that says: This too will pass.
- Listen to the tape *Is My Baby OK? Toilet Training* by Josi Alexander et al. (See **Resources**.)

Thanks to Judi Salts, Circle from Yakima, Washington

My four-year-old occasionally wets his pants and the bed. What should I do?

- Keep track of the circumstances when the accidents happen. Are the accidents happening when your child is feeling stressed? Do something to reduce the stress.
- Rule out any medical issues.
- Have him wear clothing he can manage easily himself.
- Remind him to go to the toilet just before bedtime.
- You know your child. Don't listen to people who say, "He should be trained by now."
- Know that when he is ready he will stay dry. Put diapers on him at night.
- When he wets, help him calmly get into dry clothes.
- It goes away by itself with maturation.
- Talk about how he can wake up at night and go by himself. Reassure him that you will help him if he wants it.
- Don't worry about the night at all. It is not considered at all abnormal until after six years. Ask your doctor about sphincter exercises. They are simple and they work.

Thanks to Judy Popp, Circle from Yakima, Washington

We were on vacation and returned to find our three-and-a-half-year-old talking baby talk again. How can I get her to speak as well as I know she can?

- Expect your child to regress a bit when you go away. It's her way of handling a difficult situation.
- Don't blame yourself.
- Tell her you are glad she is your daughter. Give her lots of Being affirmations. (See page 16.)
- Spend time with her doing whatever she wants every day for ten minutes.
- Give her some extra attention when she isn't talking baby talk.
- Tell her to speak clearly and that you will not respond to her baby talk. Follow through.
- Say you don't understand her. Ask her to repeat it in words you can understand.
- Don't worry about it. You know she is capable of speaking well. She will do so again when she is ready.
- It is common for three-year-olds to experiment with speech. They like to try baby talk and silly talk. Listen for ways you can join her in making a game of it.

Thanks to Deane Gradous, Circle from Minnetonka, Minnesota

E. Responsibility

My three-and-a-half-year-old is very slow in dressing herself, and sometimes it is easier to dress her myself. I want to reward her for finishing on time, and I need some ideas.

- Reward her with special attention time. Read her a story, play with her, sing songs, go for a bird-watching walk, blow bubbles together.
- Consider what time of day it is. For instance, if it is early you could give her a choice for breakfast.
- Don't set that up as hassle time.
- Make sure clothes are easy to put on.
- Expect your three-year-old to dawdle because she has so many things to find out about while she's dressing.
- Break her dressing into small parts with a raisin or Cheerio reward for each part completed.
- Set the timer and when it rings, you finish dressing her, gently but firmly.
- Relax and use this time as a special, unhurried time between you two to listen and talk to each other.
- Some days she just may not feel up to dressing herself. You won't ruin her if you dress her.
- Let her choose her own clothes.
- On days when it's important to you to get out of the house fast, just dress her.
- I ask my daughter each morning who she wants to dress her, and I allow her to pick out her clothes. I let her know the time limits.

Thanks to Melanie Weiss, Circle from Bellevue, Washington

How do I get my child to pick up his toys?

- Tell the child you will close your eyes and he can surprise you by picking up toys. Ask him to tell you when you can open your eyes for the surprise.
- Be direct, insist, and offer to help.
- Don't use "will you" or "would you" so he can say "no." Say, "It's time to pick up your toys now."
- Choose a special record that you play only at pickup time.
- Read *Four Hundred-One Ways to Get Your Kids to Work at Home* by Bonnie McCullough and Susan Monson. (See **Resources**.)
- Say, "I'll pick them up and keep them until tomorrow. If you pick them up, you can play with them again today if you wish."
- Divide the work and help. Let him know which parts are his and which parts are yours.
- Reward your child after he picks up by having everyone in the family clap and cheer.
- Get the toys picked up when the task is small. Don't wait until a million toys are strewn around.
- Read him the Berenstains' book entitled *The Berenstain Bears and the Messy Room*, and help him organize his toys. (See **Resources**.)
- Rotate toys. Keep most of them hidden away. Bring a few out at a time. They will seem new and exciting, and there will be fewer to pick up.

Thanks to Mary Ellen O'Keefe, Circle from Bellevue, Washington

My four-and-a-half-year-old has three tasks to do after breakfast: dress, brush her teeth, and feed the cat. But she doesn't do them. Rewarding with a star doesn't work any more. What can I do?

- Three things at one time may be too much for her. Give her one job at a time.
- Ask the child what she wants for a reward.
- Give her ample time and praise her for each small step.
- Change to a new reward system. Try a new kind of sticker, the use of a new toy, or an art project.
- After breakfast, ring a bell for chore time.
- Give occasional rewards. Too many rewards lose their effectiveness.
- Establish six tasks and rotate three for each week. Let her pick the three.
- Don't expect her to do it perfectly.
- Tell her she is capable of doing the task, and tell her when you want it done.
- Establish a chore list for each member of the family, and let her see how different people handle their responsibilities.

Thanks to Gail Davenport, Circle from Lynnwood, Washington

My three- and six-year-olds are yelling at and hitting the dog. What should I do?

- Make sure you or other adults aren't yelling and hitting your children. Model gentleness.
- Your kids are learning about power. Give them dog-care responsibilities: feeding the dog, walking him, or letting him in and out.
- Watch with your children a TV program about a dog and talk about how people on the show handle the dog.
- Say, "Dogs are living beings and shouldn't be hit."
- If you yell at or hit the dog, expect your kids to do the same.
- Compliment them when they are kind to the dog.
- Show and tell them exactly how you want them to interact with the dog.
- Keep them apart for now.
- Go to a dog training class, and teach your children what you learn.
- Play dog with your kids. Take turns being dog and master, so they know how it feels to be a dog.
- Don't let the kids hurt the dog. Set limits and hold to them.

Thanks to Gail Davenport, Circle from Lynnwood, Washington

What can I do about my five-and-a-half-year-old who "forgets" her backpack regularly for school?

- Help her make a picture list of the stuff she needs for school and post it on the door.
- The night before, have her put her backpack by the door.
- You are making her problem yours. Keep out of it.
- Ask her if she really needs to carry her backpack to school.
- Speak about the backpack when you and she are feeling great and not in the morning when you are in a hurry.
- Say, "Remembering your school things is your responsibility. I will not be taking them to school for you." Stick to it.
- Ask her if she wants help in remembering and what kind of help she needs.

Thanks to Ellen Peterson, Circle from Walnut Creek, California

Our four-year-old daughter will be a flower girl in a wedding. What can I do to help her?

- Have a written time schedule for you to follow and have a place for her to play a quiet game till just before her part.
- Play wedding beforehand with veil, wedding march, and bouquet so she knows what to expect. Let her play different roles.
- Remember, she doesn't have to be perfect. People will love her anyway.
- Invent a signal system with her so she can look to you for a signal if she needs reassurance.
- Put a quarter where your little girl is to stand. When the ceremony is over she can have the quarter.
- Put Cheerios in the basket for her to eat during the ceremony.
- Be sure she is included in the rehearsal and walk her through it several times. Children don't learn as fast as adults.
- Enjoy it with her; she'll be wonderful.

Thanks to Marilyn Grevstad, Circle from Seattle, Washington

How can I encourage my kids to be cautious of strangers without being fearful of strangers?

- Make a rule like: If you don't know the person, come and ask Mom or Dad about them.
- Start talking now about the good or bad qualities of people, rather than good or bad people.
- Since some children are shy and some are outgoing, make rules that fit each child.
- Role-play with them different situations and what they would do and how they would feel. Don't overdo it.
- Teach them, if lost, to find a cash register and ask the person there to help them. Walk them through it.
- Discuss out loud how you as an adult look at strangers and check with your feelings to decide whether you can trust them.
- Get some good books for kids on this subject: *Private Zone* by Frances Dayee, *Safety Zone* by Linda Meyer, *Jenny's New Game* by Laurella Cross, and *It's My Body* by Lory Freeman. Remember this takes time to learn. They won't learn it overnight. (See **Resources**.)
- Look at this as another "safety rule" that we teach our children, just as we teach them about "safety rules" in crossing the street.

(See also I-4.)

Thanks to Christine Ternand, Circle from Minneapolis, Minnesota

F. Coping with Special Stresses

Since her father left last month, my four-year-old resists bedtime. How can I avoid threats and help her at bedtime?

- In the morning say, "Tonight I will read you two stories at bedtime and kiss you goodnight." Then do it and leave her room.
- Realize that this is emotionally difficult for your child as well as for you. Give her extra hugs at night. Rock her if she likes.
- Let her know that however she feels about the absence of her father is OK.
- Rock her and sing the Being affirmations. (See page 16.)
- Encourage her to watch *Mister Rogers* on TV.
- Reassure her that you will not leave.
- See if she wants her door open and let her have a night light.
- Instead of sending her off to bed, you put her to bed.
- Don't threaten. Talk gently and carry her to bed.
- Go to a Parents Without Partners meeting and ask how other parents have handled this. (For information, write: Parents Without Partners, Inc., 7910 Woodmount Ave., Bethesda, Maryland 20614.)
- Lie down beside her and read a story.
- Set the bedtime and tell her, "In fifteen minutes we will start your bedtime routine." Then do it in fifteen minutes.

Thanks to Margot Tobias, Circle from Walnut Creek, California

My child doesn't want to go to preschool without me. What can I do?

• Play out this school situation with him with small people figures to familiarize him with the routine.
• Join a carpool so he can be friends with the other children.
• Ask him what special things he would like to do in preschool. Try to arrange it.
• Observe the preschool to find possible reasons for his not wanting to go.
• Talk to him about how he feels and let him know you believe he can handle preschool.
• If you can, try a different preschool.
• Give him lots of recognition and encouragement.
• Have some of his school friends over to your house to play.
• Consider the possibility that he may not be ready for preschool.
• If he *has* to go because you need him cared for at that time, tell him.
• Many three-year-olds kick up a fuss but play quite happily once Mother is out of sight.

(See also **Preparing Your Child for Grade School.**)

Thanks to Ellen Peterson, Circle from Walnut Creek, California

What do I do when my child comes home from preschool wiped out, has tantrums, screams, or is demanding?

- Be ready for her when she comes. Give her your attention without demands for ten minutes.
- Your daughter may be just learning how to make transitions. Give her time.
- Pick her up at school and make the ride home a nice transition time, with soothing music and pleasant talk.
- Rock her and sing to her or lie down for a short rest time together.
- Let the tantrum run its course, and when it's over, offer to rock her.
- You could check out the possibility of abuse. Ask other parents if their children also have behavior problems. (See page 10.)
- Don't make demands of someone in a rebellious state. It won't work.
- Hug her and say, "I'm glad to see you."
- Consider cutting down on the number of days she attends school for now.
- Maybe the experience is too demanding. Read David Elkind's book, *The Hurried Child*. (See **Resources**.)
- Meet her with food.
- Shorten the length of time she is at preschool, if you can.

(See also **Ages and Stages**.)

Thanks to Nat Houtz, Circle from Lacey, Washington

My three-and-a-half-year-old throws tantrums when we come to get him after he has been playing at someone's house.

- Prearrange a departure routine. For example, put on his sweater and have him say good-bye to the dog.
- Say, "Wow, I'm glad you had a good time. Let's figure out when we can do it again." Make a date before leaving.
- Call ten minutes before to give him the "ten minute get ready."
- Have someone else pick him up for you.
- Hug him and say, "I'm glad to see you."
- At another time ask him what he needs to come home easily.
- Allow him to assert his independence in this way.
- Acknowledge his feelings about not wanting to leave.
- Set time limits for the fussing. Then pick him up and go.
- Visualize a good experience. See Clarke's *Self-Esteem: A Family Affair* for ideas about visualization. (See **Resources**.)
- Allow time to play with him there.
- Remind yourself that this is a sign that he feels safe expressing his emotions with you.
- Ignore the screaming, make sure he's safe, and know that this behavior is common for kids this age.

Thanks to Ellen Peterson, Circle from Walnut Creek, California

How can I prepare my kids to go somewhere without getting hassled?

- Give them a warning, "We're leaving in ten minutes." Then when it's time, announce, "We're leaving." Honor your word to leave when you say you will.
- Say, "I'm starting to get ready," and then have a race with them.
- The night before have them choose and take out the clothes they will wear and get their belongings ready.
- Give them a warning prior to leaving. Set consequences and when the timer dings, follow through.
- Relax. It's OK to be late sometimes. Kids this age dawdle.
- Getting ready may have lots of parts. Help the children identify the parts, then reward each one.
- Give them a reward if they are ready early.
- Allow lots of time for yourself to get ready.
- If they are not ready when it is time to go to preschool, take them in pajamas with their clothes in a sack.
- Make a rule that they are not to leave their room in the morning until they are dressed.
- Be calm.
- Visualize your chldren being ready on time.

Thanks to Sue Hansen, Circle from Bellevue, Washington

My son leaves a store yelling and screaming because he wanted all the items he saw. What can I do?

- Tell him, "no," ignore the screaming, and leave.
- Before going tell him, "I have this much to spend on you today."
- Give him a piggy bank and pennies to save for the store.
- Before you go, tell him matter-of-factly about something specific that *you* want that you will not be getting.
- Make sure it's a good time to go to the store— when neither of you is tired, hungry, or emotionally drained.
- Prepare him in the car by telling him what items you will be looking for, and tell him what behavior you expect from him.
- While at the store make a wish-list to have for special occasions and birthdays.
- Be consistent about times when he gets to choose items and when he doesn't, and decide before you go into the store.
- Say, "I choose not to buy that for you right now."
- Don't take him with you. Get someone to watch him.
- Remind yourself that the media bombard all of us with messages to buy more.

(See also A-7.)

Thanks to Pearl Noreen, Circle from Seattle, Washington

G. Picky Eaters

I have a four-year-old who eats very slowly. What can I do about it?

- Let him time himself with a stop watch, and try to reduce his time each day.
- Give him very small portions (one teaspoon) to begin with. If he's still hungry, he will ask for more.
- Have him serve himself. Accept his choices.
- Don't let him snack close to dinner time.
- Honor his pace and say, "When you have had enough, you may take your plate to the sink."
- Research shows slow eaters are much less likely to have weight problems.
- Some children are slow eaters. If he seems to enjoy his meal, even though he eats slowly, allow him the time to do so.
- Consider whether you need to be together as a family at mealtime. See if having him eat separately makes it easier for him to attend to eating.
- Give him a head start. Provide him something to nibble prior to dinner so part of his eating is done before you start.
- When *you* are done, excuse yourself and let him finish.
- Drop your membership in the "Clean-Your-Plate Club" and when others are through, take his plate whether he's finished or not.

Thanks to Betty Beach, Circle from Minnetonka, Minnesota

My child does not eat at the evening meal. I am worried about her nutrition. What can I do?

• Have fun things to eat with, like a huge spoon, toothpicks, tongs.

• Remember that many children eat in cycles at this age—a month of eating well and a month of eating like a bird.

• Put an array of healthy food on a buffet and let her serve herself and eat what she wants.

• Don't worry. She can get what she needs from breakfast and lunch.

• Invite the child to help you cook, and offer her tastes as you go.

• Routinely prepare a vegetable or fruit snack one and one-half hours before dinner and no eating after that until dinner.

• No snacks between lunch and dinner. Hunger is your best ally.

• Have a dinner time when she needs it (at her own time, not necessarily the rest of the family's).

• Do not allow toys at the table.

• Don't fix special food just for her.

• Let her help plan some menus. Teach her to include a protein, vegetable, and starch.

• Examine the atmosphere at the dinner table. Is it enjoyable for her?

Thanks to Marilyn Grevstad, Circle from Seattle, Washington

How can I get my children to stay at the dinner table?

- Tell them this is eating time. Set the timer for ten minutes and when it dings, clear their food and let them get down.
- Use a special plate that means "You're the Special Person of the Day."
- Let the children choose what they want to eat (within reasonable limits).
- Evaluate your mealtime. Is it when the children aren't hungry or are so tired they can't concentrate?
- Have "special" dinners (perhaps foods from other countries) and include the children in preparing table decorations—specially folded napkins, place cards, etc.
- Tell them when they leave the table they are finished eating. No more food till breakfast.
- Make sure they have comfortable chairs where they can see what's going on.
- Play "restaurant" in which you use your best table manners, dress up, and set out good dishes.
- It's impossible for most kids to sit still very long.
- Serve food in muffin tins or on doll dishes.
- Why is it important to you? Tell your child why.

Thanks to Marilyn Grevstad, Circle from Seattle, Washington

My child is always asking for candy, and I don't want her having very much of it. What can I do?

- On Saturday, let her choose three pieces from a jar of candy, and make it clear that Saturday is the only day you will give her candy.
- Don't buy it. Say no. It's OK for her to be angry, if she wants to.
- Buy individually wrapped snacks like cheese cubes. Part of the fun of candy is opening little packages.
- Ask your dentist to talk with her and use visual aids.
- At the store let her choose her favorite nonsugar snacks for the week.
- Tell her what you know about sugar. List the effects.
- Don't let her watch TV! It is loaded with candy advertisements.
- Together, make nutritious snacks like whole-grain cookies with raisins, granola bars, or yogurt popsicles.
- Tell her, "We don't have or eat candy in our house." Be sure you follow that rule too.
- I'll be interested to see when you ask for stickers instead of candy.
- Give her hugs instead.

Thanks to Melanie Weiss, Circle from Bellevue, Washington

My five-and-a-half-year-old declares himself a vegetarian for a week every once in a while. What should I do?

- This is a personal preference issue. Meat is not the only source of protein. Check out other high-protein foods.
- If it helps you feel better, make sure he takes vitamins.
- Read Frances Lappe's *Diet for a Small Planet* and offer him lots of fresh fruits and vegetables. (See **Resources**.)
- If he continues to be a vegetarian longer than one or two weeks, check out his diet with your doctor or a dietician. Growing children may need supplements not normally noted in vegetarian guide books.
- Take him to McDonald's, and he'll probably decide vegetarianism isn't so hot.
- Listen to him. He's a smart kid! That's a healthy way to eat.
- Don't make an issue of it.
- Respect his ideas and involve him in exploring different options or meal preparations.
- Use cashew butter, almond butter, and peanut butter.

Thanks to Becky Monson, Circle from Minnetonka, Minnesota

H. Things to Do

What can I do with my preschooler on a rainy day?

- Get the book *Rainy Day Activities for Preschoolers*, by the Mercer Island Preschool Association. (See **Resources**.)
- Don't resort to TV. Instead, develop a rainy day routine. For example, on rainy days we can wear pajamas till 11:00, then we have a picnic in the laundry room, then we go for an umbrella walk.
- Cook together—make fancy hors d'oeuvres.
- Keep a box of toys and art materials hidden away just for rainy days.
- Invite another preschooler over to play and get out a box of dress-up clothes. Anything will do, even cut- off pant legs or sleeves. Kids love being silly.
- For some part of the day say, "You know where your toys are. You decide what you will do while I read my book."
- Allow her to play with water at the sink. Add food coloring or bubbles.
- Scrub the kitchen floor together.
- Take a trip to the library for books, records, and tapes. Then snuggle down together for a listening time.
- Build spaceships with whatever—blocks, furniture, pillows, boxes, or blankets.
- Use real sewing things. You can sew together.

(See also H-2.)

Thanks to Carole Gesme, Circle from Minneapolis, Minnesota

How can you keep three- and four-year-olds entertained and help them enjoy the ride when carpooling to preschool and home?

- Plan the seating arrangement for peace! You decide.
- Play song and story tapes. (*Wee Sing Play Book and Cassette* by Beall and Nipp is good.) Bring granola bars or grapes.
- Give stickers for good behavior.
- Play games: I Spy with My Little Eye, The Alphabet Game, I'm Thinking of . . . , Rhyming Words.
- Sing or tell stories.
- Ask about: Jobs people do, weather, seasons, holidays, preschool events, and enjoy the children's answers. If there is a favorite seat, rotate who sits in it.
- Look for things: motorcycles, stop signs, water towers, fire hydrants, VW Bugs.

Thanks to Gail Davenport, Circle from Lynnwood, Washington

I will be driving across the country with my daughters, ages twenty-four months and four and one half years. I would like traveling tips.

- Attach a shoe bag to the back seat or some other part of the car. This is a handy place to store toys and snacks and a way to keep toddler training cups full of juice.
- Contact AAA to map a route with rest stops marked.
- Take turns in different seats in the car. Rearrange the children and parents a couple of times each day.
- Take along a cassette recorder with story tapes for the children and a blank tape for recording your own sing-along.
- Give fruit for a snack. It's juicy and won't make the children thirsty like most other snacks.
- Gift wrap an assortment of small toys and activities. Open one periodically. They don't have to be new toys.
- Don't try to cover too many miles at once. Break the trip into short sections of travel each day, making frequent exercise stops.
- Try to arrange your seating so one adult can focus on one child.
- Make a felt board on an old record jacket with felt pieces to stick on.

(See also H-2.)

Thanks to Gail Davenport, Circle from Alderwood, Washington

How can I prepare my child for a move?

• Ask him to choose some favorite things to keep out and carry with him in his suitcase. Let him help pack the rest.
• Pack his things last.
• Help him say good-bye to his room, the kitchen, the yard, etc.
• Read him the Berenstain Bears' book on moving. (See **Resources**.)
• Tell him you love him and give him lots of hugs. Attending to your child is more important than having things packed perfectly.
• Tell him why you are moving. Mark moving day on a big calendar.
• Make time for fun. Have a going-away party with his friends and give each your new address.
• If he cries about leaving, let him cry.
• Use a babysitter while you are packing.
• Show on a map where you will be moving, and let him follow the route. If driving or flying, have a little celebration as you cross each state line.
• Don't use this time to throw away his old toys. Preschoolers are very attached to "things."
• Give him pictures of the new house and a picture of the old house to take.

Thanks to Pearl Noreen, Circle from Seattle, Washington

How can I help my child wait for a big event that is a month away?

- Don't tell him about it too far in advance, if possible.
- Make a paper chain with a link for each day until the event, and remove a link each day.
- Don't talk about it all the time.
- Change the focus from what's in it for him to what he can do for others—making gifts, wrapping them, decorating the house.
- Say, "It really is hard to wait. Let's make a list of three things you can do to get ready."
- Draw pictures of what he imagines is going to happen. You could draw too. Decorate the room with the pictures.
- Plan tiny weekly events to prepare for the big event.
- Try to de-emphasize it. Keep routines normal.
- Have your child mark off or put a sticker on the calendar as each day passes so he can keep track.

Thanks to Ellen Peterson, Circle from Alamo, California

I. Bodies and Sex

My five-year-old was playing with a friend in the bedroom. My husband opened the door and found them masturbating. Our rule is that that behavior is OK for our son _alone_ in his bedroom. We need suggestions for appropriate consequences for breaking that rule.

- Be honest with your son about your feelings.
- After the friend has left, tell your son not to forget the rule again.
- Do not allow the kids to play in the bedroom with the door closed.
- Review your rules about private parts to him. Don't impose special consequences now, unless he knew them ahead of time.
- Don't blame yourself or think your son is bad. He is just trying to learn about bodies. Treat it seriously but don't take it seriously.
- You could decide on some consequences to give if it happened again. Say, "You can't play in your bedroom with a friend for two days."
- Matter-of-factly tell them both they have broken the family rule and not to break it again.
- Send his friend home.
- Don't send the friend home. It will make it seem like they've committed a crime.

(See also **Time-Out**.)

Thanks to Sue Hansen, Circle from Bellevue, Washington

My five-year-old daughter touches the private parts of mannequins in department stores. She lifts clothing and looks. What can I do?

- Say, "You may not do this."
- Get her a set of dolls with genitals and set the rule that it is OK to explore at home, but not in public.
- Go with her to check out some mannequins. She's *just* curious.
- Be honest that this is embarrassing to you and that you expect her not to play with mannequins in stores.
- Check museums or children's museums for displays of body parts. Take her to see them.
- Together read *Where Did I Come From?* by Peter Mayle and giggle over the pictures. (See **Resources**.)
- Ask your doctor if she has any models of body parts.
- Bathe together and use this as an opportunity to talk about bodies.
- Remember, it's OK to be curious.

Thanks to Sue Hansen, Circle from Bellevue, Washington

My five-year-old son stayed overnight at the home of some five- and eight-year-old friends. His friends were inserting their penises into each other's anuses and trying to urinate. My son was resistant but finally was coerced and really enjoyed it. He came home excited and wanted to teach his three-year-old brother. I don't want to teach him his body is dirty. How can I stop this behavior?

- Approach it from a hygiene angle. Say, "It is not a clean place to put your penis. It is the body's wastes that are unclean, not your body." Don't overreact. Kids are very interested in bodies at this age. Read Joe Kaufman's *How We Are Born, How We Grow, How Our Bodies Work, and How We Learn.* (See **Resources**.)
- Say, "Your brother has private parts of his body that you may not touch."
- Compliment your son on resisting. Then read Lory Freeman's *It's My Body* with him. (See **Resources**.)
- Say, "That probably did feel good, but don't do this with other boys. Sex is between adults. It is something special you will enjoy when you are older."
- Talk with the other parents. Let them know what their kids are doing.
- You're doing well to keep communication open.

Thanks to Melanie Weiss, Circle from Bellevue, Washington

How do you handle a four-year-old girl who is overly interested in sex? The child was sexually molested by her grandfather and others. She tries to play with the genitals of her three-year-old friend and men we know, and she lies on the floor and spreads her legs.

- Take care of your own feelings about this. Get counseling support for yourself and for her.
- Make sure she has lots of active kids to play with.
- Watch her and compliment her for appropriate play with the friend.
- Read her *It's My Body* by Lory Freeman. (See **Resources**.)
- When she lies on the floor, get her up and get her started in a new activity.
- Enroll her in tumbling or swimming classes to help her appreciate her body.
- Give her a lot of love.
- Say, "I will not allow people to touch you in your private places, and I won't allow you to do that to others."
- Children who have been sexually molested frequently confuse sexual touch for love or think that sexual behavior is the only way to get love. Be sure she gets lots of holding, rocking, wrestling, and other appropriate touching.
- Keep her away from her grandfather.

(See also **Where to Go for Additional Support**.)

Thanks to Sara Monser, Circle from Lafayette, California

J. Hassles with Other Adults

My parents favor my sons over my daughters. What can I do?

- Tell your parents quite frankly that this bothers you and why.
- Did they do this when *you* were little? Get in touch with your feelings about this.
- Let the girls know you are glad they are girls and let the boys know you are glad they are boys.
- Tell your parents how confusing these messages are to children who are just learning to identify their own sex.
- Ask your parents to favor your daughters also.
- Tell your children you love them.
- Every generation has its hang-ups and its gifts.
- If this bothers your children, talk to them and listen to them.
- If you think this situation is too bad, don't let them see their grandparents.
- Don't try to make your parents into something they are not.

Thanks to Carole Gesme, Circle from Anoka, Minnesota

My children sometimes go to Grandma's for a weekend. Grandma won't follow the children's schedules, and she lets them run her.

- Tell Grandma how you want things done and how you feel about what she is doing.
- You may not be able to change your in-laws. Tell them straight and decide if the price of going to Grandma's is worth it.
- Grandparents are for loving kids. Let her do it her way.
- Make sure your children are safe. If not, find someone else to keep the children.
- Listen to Jay O'Callahan's tape *The Little Dragon and Other Stories*, which is about relationships between grandmas and grandkids. (See **Resources**.)
- Write a list for Grandma. Include nap schedule, food likes, etc.
- Decide on a few things that are really important to you; insist on these and let the rest go.
- Grandmas are meant to be different from parents and are important people to your kids.
- Kids can learn there are different rules at different houses. Make sure the rules are safe and encourage them to talk about "alikes" and differences.
- Tell Grandma that you know she will be in charge and to make sure the weekend is enjoyable for her, too.

Thanks to Marilyn Grevstad, Circle from Seattle, Washington

How can I cope during a weekend stay with my in-laws, who are not very tolerant of my five-year-old son's behavior? This causes my spouse to react strongly toward our son also.

- Plan activities away from their home each day of your stay.
- Ask your husband to treat your son the same way he usually does.
- Take good care of yourself for two days before you go.
- Tell your husband why you would prefer to stay home.
- Let your son know you love him.
- Stay out of your husband's or in-law's anxiety. Make a list of "Good Parent Rules" for yourself.
- Be specific with your husband before the trip about the discipline you and he will use.
- Ask your in-laws to state the two most important rules for your son to follow at their house.
- Start them reminiscing about your husband's childhood, especially when he was five.
- If it's too intolerable, have them come to your house next time.
- Ask your son to figure out how to get along with his grandparents and father.
- Take a look at the boy's behavior. Is it normal five-year-old stuff, or does he need some training in manners?

Thanks to Deane Gradous, Circle from Wayzata, Minnesota

My boyfriend is too strict with my child. What should I do?

- Explain to him that you will handle the situation.
- If he's physically or emotionally abusive, dump him.
- Listen to his side of it. Maybe you are too lenient. Think about it and decide if it fits.
- Tell him what you want him to do.
- Don't hassle this issue in front of your child. Talk, listen, and share child-care expectations when you are away from your child. This is an issue between adults.
- Ask him how he was treated when he was her age. Tell him how you were treated and what you want for your daughter. Talk about personalities, expectations, and discipline.
- Take a parenting class together.
- Trust your child to work out her own relationship with your boyfriend.
- Get a nonbiased opinion.
- Put up a poster of normal child behaviors at this age as a reminder to you and your boyfriend.

(See also **About Abuse** and **Ages and Stages**.)

Thanks to Ellen Peterson, Circle from Lafayette, California

How can I handle the parent of a three-year-old who spanks or slaps her child in my presence in my home? I disapprove.

- You can call a child protection service.
- Tell her the rule at your house is that no one gets hit.
- Put up a sign: "People are not for hitting. Children are people."
- Share with her the section on what to do instead of hitting from Clarke's *Self-Esteem: A Family Affair*. (See **Resources**.)
- Talk to the parent about spanking at another time when the three-year-old is not present.
- My friend and I tell each other about times we feel like hitting and don't; that helps us both.
- Don't walk away. Tell her how you feel.
- Talk about how you feel like hitting sometimes and don't; let your friend see and hear how you do this with your child.
- Tell your friend all the reasons you like her. Then share your beliefs about discipline without spanking.

Thanks to Harold Nordeman, Circle from Cincinnati, Ohio

Our three-year-old son prefers me, and this disturbs his mother. How can we respond to him when she wants to give him something and he will take it only from Daddy?

- Mom can say, "Your dad's busy right now. I'm here now to give you this. If you want it, it's yours!"
- Arrange for him to have time alone with you.
- Remember, Dad, that his attachment to you is a stage and won't last forever. Have fun with him.
- Tell yourself it's not anyone's fault.
- Point out to your wife all the ways she is a good mom.
- Agree between you not to get your feelings hurt by this. Don't be manipulated.
- Say, "Hey, I really love it that you want it from me, but I'm busy right now."
- Read about triangles and family maps in *Peoplemaking* by Virginia Satir. (See **Resources**.)
- Know that it has happened in many households and kids have still grown up to love both parents.

Thanks to Craig Halversen, Circle from Coon Rapids, Minnesota

My husband, from whom I am separated, gives our three- and six-year-olds a dollar allowance for chores they do while visiting him. The children expect it from me, too, but I can't afford it. What can I do?

- Say, "We don't use the same set of rules here."
- Have some chores your children do because they are part of the family and some they can do to earn money.
- Can't blame them for giving it a try! Give each a hug and simply say you don't have the money.
- Don't give them money just because he does. Decide what you want to do and do it your way.
- Give your children the allowance *you* can afford for experience in handling money, not as a reward for chores.
- Tell them that isn't how you choose to spend your money. Your children are learning that people do things differently. That's valuable.
- Your kids love you because you're you—not because of how much allowance you give.
- Teach them about other types of rewards.
- Say, "Your dad and I do this differently. It's OK for you to love us both."

Thanks to Linda Witt, Circle from Cincinnati, Ohio

How do I get my husband to help with the house and the kids?

- Be specific. Don't say, "I want help." Say exactly what you want and write it down.
- Use *fair* delegation. Let him be responsible for things he enjoys. Split jobs you both hate.
- Point out how you will both benefit when he helps. You will have a better disposition, and he and the kids will know each other better.
- Get mad.
- Discuss the roles of both parents. Ask him what he expects a dad to do. Your ideas may not be the same. Negotiate a compromise.
- Be flexible. Sometimes I don't feel like doing much and sometimes he doesn't. Trade off.
- When I feel desperate, I say, "It's your turn and I mean it."
- Don't talk about it when you're heated up. Go away someplace and talk about it.
- Go off by yourself.
- List all the things to be done. Together decide which ones he will do.

Thanks to Sara Monser, Circle from Lafayette, California

My day-care person won't let my three-year-old son wear the women's clothes from the dress-up closet. I think it's OK.

• Talk to the day-care person directly and tell her that it's OK with you.
• Ask her why and listen to her reasons.
• Explain to your son that some people don't understand that kids like to dress up all kinds of ways. Make sure he has dress-up clothes at home.
• Check out another day care.
• Let him wear something special from home so he can feel "dressed-up."
• Tell the provider, "He has a great imagination. Kids can pretend to be anything they want. Pretending doesn't make things come true. Some days he pretends he is a dinosaur. Please let him wear all of the dress-ups."
• I used to feel funny about my son dressing up, too, until I read *Growing Up Free* by Letty Pogrebin. Give it to her. (See **Resources**.)
• Tell your provider to please let him have free access to the dress-up closet but to please let you know if he does it to the exclusion of other play.

Thanks to Sara Monser, Circle from Lafayette, California

K. Parents Have Needs, Too

When is my time? How do I get my child to respect my right to be with friends and on the phone?

- Make it clear when you will spend time just with him and when you will spend time talking to adults. Give him his time first.
- Stop and talk to him. Explain your need to talk to adults.
- Keep some special quiet toys by the phone, to be played with only while you're talking.
- You are important. Arrange with your neighbor to watch your child while you are with friends or want a long phone conversation.
- Don't be too long on the phone. Save long talks for naptime.
- Don't always answer the phone. Tell the child you are choosing to be with him instead.
- Reward the child with hugs for a few minutes of quiet while you are on the phone.
- Help your child arrange a special time with a friend and tell him when you have special arrangements with your friends.
- Congratulate yourself on having a healthy child who is pushing you and others to find out what the limits are and how he can be part of the action.
- Meet a friend at the park and talk while the kids play. They are happy, and you are happy!

Thanks to Sandy Keiser, Circle from Cincinnati, Ohio

Our three-year-old daughter and seventeen-month-old son climb onto the pool table where I keep my Avon samples. How can I keep them off?

- Keep pulling them off. State the rule of staying off.
- Establish private places for each member of the family to keep their stuff. Remind the children.
- You deserve your own space. Claim it!
- Set up an alternative climbing apparatus or trampoline nearby to climb on.
- Remember that you establish rules differently for different ages. Change the environment for the toddler and make consequences for the three-year-old.
- Could you build a cover of plywood to set over the pool table and Avon samples?
- Get them their own Avon samples or little jars and lids, and remind them to play with their own samples, not yours.
- Find a new space, like a cupboard, that you can lock. It isn't safe for little ones to eat your products. Protect your children.

Thanks to Marilyn Grevstad, Circle from Seattle, Washington

I am too busy. I feel guilty about my busy scheduled days and worry that my child is not getting enough of my attention. What can I do?

- Make a list of tasks, prioritize them, and include some time for yourself and for your child each day.
- Find a good preschool, where your child can have fun and get lots of attention from other people. Work fast while she is gone and give her attention while she is home.
- Pay attention to your own feelings and needs as well as other people's.
- My mom worked, and I learned lots from watching her, listening to her stories about her work, and figuring out how to get things done.
- It's OK to say no. You don't have to do it all now.
- Don't stay in "worry." Look at your choices and decide what is best for you and your child in your situation at this time.
- Instead of thinking "only two hours," think "I've got two hours and that's lots of time."
- Look at your old "good mom rules." Rewrite them to work for you now. Read more about this in Clarke's *Self-Esteem: A Family Affair*. (See **Resources**.)
- Invite the child to help you at meetings by getting ready and serving refreshments, etc.
- Foster a spirit of cooperation.

Thanks to Susie Montgomery, Circle from Lafayette, California

My in-laws criticize me a lot. How can I not feel condemned? They will be spending ten days with me.

- Don't forget, this is their point of view, and you can say, "Thank you, I'll think about that."
- Say, "I don't do things the way you do. There are lots of different ways of doing things. This is the way I'm doing it now."
- Say to yourself, "I am a duck and this criticism is so much water off my back."
- Tell them to stop it.
- Remove yourself and think of a response you can give next time. Rehearse.
- Whenever you feel threatened, use centering and leveling techniques. Stand and sit straight and breathe deeply. Read *The Centering Book* by Gay Hendricks. (See **Resources**.)
- Say, "I feel hurt when you say that. Please tell me about something I do well."
- Write an affirmation for yourself, give it to a friend, and ask her to read it to you when you call. Call once every day and listen. (See page 14.)
- Keep a list of the things they do that bother you. When you are an in-law, do something else.
- Remember, children deserve to hear their parents honored, not abused. If the criticism is too much for you or your children to tolerate, ask your in- laws to leave.

Thanks to Cindy Vernatter, Circle from Cincinnati, Ohio

What about me? As my child practices the independence I am fostering, I no longer feel needed.

- Say to yourself, "Isn't this neat? This is what I'm working for."
- Ask a friend for a hug and celebrate your success with your child.
- You will always be needed, but the ways in which you are needed will change.
- Think of how your own needs change in time.
- Take care of the child in you! Start a new hobby, buy yourself a present, or take a friend to lunch.
- It's OK to mourn the loss of your child's babyhood.
- Write a letter to yourself about this new experience and what you feel, and read it whenever you need to.
- Think about your child at age nine, fifteen, and twenty-three and how you would feel if he were not independent.
- Read the adult affirmations to yourself morning and night for three weeks and then see how you feel.

Thanks to Mary Paananen, Circle from Seattle, Washington

The clod and I are getting a divorce. How can I prepare my child?

- Prepare your child by giving some facts as they occur rather than letting it out all at once.
- Get some help for yourself so you can say something other than "the clod." Find ways to let out your feelings that do not involve your daughter.
- Provide opportunities for her to associate with other loving adults and with children who have survived divorce.
- Tell the child's teacher.
- Continue as much of your regular routine as possible and structure some high-quality times with your child.
- Tell her, "When we got married we loved each other very much. Now our love for each other has changed, but love for children doesn't change. We will continue to love you."
- Say, "Though things are changing, you are important and we will always be your mom and dad."
- Say, "This is not your fault. Big people get divorces for their own reasons. Little people do not cause them."
- Tell her about the future—where she will be living, with whom, about visitations, etc.
- Take care of yourself and do the best you can. Remember you don't have to be perfect.

Thanks to Mary Paananen, Circle from Seattle, Washington

I have just moved here. How do I find new friends?

- Find a church to attend and volunteer to help.
- Take a fun class. Pick one that might attract people who like to do things you enjoy.
- Go on outings: fairs, hikes, community holiday celebrations and festivals, and talk to people.
- Be active in groups involving kids: La Leche League, school, preschool, Sunday school, parenting class.
- See if there is a babysitting co-op. Ask parents in grocery stores, parks, etc., and if you can't find one, start one.
- Pursue a hobby—bowling, flower arranging, playing an instrument—and find a group to do it with.
- Join a preschool, babysitting, or food co-op.
- Stay around after meetings or classes. That is when people get to know each other more personally.
- Offer to teach a skill you have.
- After a meeting or class, invite the group to your house for coffee.
- I remember that lonely feeling. Taking care of *you* is more important than unpacking all the boxes.

Thanks to Sandra Sittko, Circle from St. Louis, Missouri

What should I look for in choosing a preschool?

- Take your child's personality and needs into consideration.
- If you want to be involved, look for a cooperative preschool. You can take your time and find one that's just right for you and your child or start one yourself. (See page 116.)
- Look for a preschool in which social skills will be learned. This is an important task for preschool children.
- Look for a preschool in which the child will have fun. Don't worry about academics yet.
- Look for invitations to participate but no forced activities.
- Check on these things: the teachers' credentials, reputation, the schedule (time outdoors, etc.), the adults-to-child ratio, who watches the kids, whether parents are welcome, meals, field trips, outside specialists, amount of indoor climbing equipment, the cleanliness of the school, and how they handle sick children.
- Listen to the opinions of friends who share your values.
- Is the discipline positive or negative?
- Observe the children. Are they happy? Are they listless? Are they out of control?

(See also **Preparing Your Child for Grade School**.)

Thanks to Marilyn Grevstad, Circle from Seattle, Washington

Time-Out

What Is Time-Out?

Time-out is a technique used to interrupt unacceptable behavior by removing the child from the "scene of the action." Time-out is a calming device, not a punishment.

When and Where to Use It

Use time-out for stopping inappropriate behavior before it reaches oppressive or assaultive proportions or for serious violations of your family's rules. Put the child in a safe, boring place within your view.

The time-out should be short enough so the child has many chances to go back to the original situation and learn acceptable behavior (a minute or less for young children).

Procedure

Before using a time-out, see if your child understands the concepts of "wait" and "quiet." (Children usually do between two-and-a-half and three-and-a-half years.) Then choose an appropriate location for time-out.

The first few times, do this:
1. Explain a time-out to the child.
2. Explain when it will be used.
3. Walk the child through the steps (when a rule has been broken).

4. Time the quiet time only (not whining or crying).
5. Tell the child the time-out is over when the time is up.
6. Return the child to the situation and reinforce appropriate behavior.

This summary of the time-out strategy is from Elizabeth Crary's *Without Spanking or Spoiling*. (See **Resources**.) See her book for a more complete description of the uses and pitfalls of using time-outs.

—The Editors

Preparing Your Child for Grade School

All the parents I know would like their children to be at the top of their class. We all want our kids to bring home the gold stars. However, most of our kids, like us, will be somewhere in between the top and the bottom. That's OK, because there are lots of gifted children in the world and some have gifts that comply with school ideals and some have gifts that shine elsewhere.

The preschool years are a time when children get to know themselves in relation to other people in the world. It is a time of preparation for "school age." Parents who are thinking ahead ask, "How can I help my children succeed in elementary school? Is there some way I can give them a head start?"

As a preschool teacher, I notice that very bright children often have advanced verbal skills. They may learn to count at an early age; they may learn their colors at an early age; they may memorize the alphabet at an early age. Parents sometimes mistake these verbal indicators as *causes* of intelligence. "If only I can get someone to teach my child ABCs, colors, and counting, he will be bright too." Then preschool panic sets in and parents want to push.

Pushing doesn't help. Don't push your children into learning about symbols before they are ready. If you do, they will develop a distaste for numbers and letters. Let *them* lead *you* down the academic road. Respond to their questions about letters and numbers just as you do to other questions about what life is about. That's all the teaching you need to do.

Don't send them to a pushy preschool. They'll learn to hate learning and think of school as a place where grown-ups make them do things they don't want to do. Preschool should be fun.

See your children as the very capable persons they already are. All things in their own good time. You can help your children more if you rejoice in what they have already learned about the world, their neighborhood, their family and friends, and above all themselves. They have already accomplished quite a lot in a very short time.

Love them and believe in them. Children do better in school when they see themselves as lovable and capable. When parents believe their children are lovable and capable, their sons and daughters believe it too.

Give your children lots of hands-on learning experiences, things in which they use ther bodies as well as their minds. Help them engage fully with life. To do this, provide as many of those activities traditionally loved by preschoolers as you can. That way, your children will have had a rich array of experiences before they begin formal schooling. These experiences will develop the basic skills that support learning the "basic skills." To support this process, you can provide these:

sand	pretend-play props
water	glue and stuff to glue
paper	scissors
paints	markers, pencils, pens
playdough	friends
clay and mud	books and stories
climbers	swings
musical instruments	field trips to stores
records, songs	banks, doctors, parks
wheel toys	outdoor time

Good preschools can be a great benefit. The best kind are those in which children have long periods of time to play with each other and the above materials. Parents who can share their preschoolers' enthusiasm for life will be able to provide many experiences, materials, and field trips for their children without benefit of preschool, but preschool does add many experiences hard to duplicate at home, with the addition of groups of children to play with.

Preschool does not have to be expensive. Cooperative preschools are usually low in cost because parents provide staff help. Many parents form play groups where several children rotate from house to house and parents take turns being host/teacher. This is an excellent way to provide preschool at almost no cost. Most day-care centers include a preschool program.

If you choose to send your children to preschool or kindergarten, find a school that fits your children, rather than expecting your children to mold to the expectations of the school. This kind of compliance is difficult for a child and may result in lowered self-esteem.

If your children are quite active and love to climb, find a school that includes running and climbing as part of the curriculum. They will feel good about themselves and will be willing to learn new things once they have had their fill of active play. If one of your children is quite shy, find a school with a minimum of pressure to perform in front of a group. When allowed to do his own thing unobtrusively, your shy child will in time feel safe, and ready to warm up to the supportive adults and friendly children who are around. In other words, find a school that will allow your children to be who they are and that will offer them new experiences as well.

Two helpful things you can do for children at home are to read to them and to talk to them. Books to own and regular trips to the library for interesting books will help them develop a love of reading. (When ready, sometime between six and nine, they will learn *how* to read.) When you talk to children, you build their vocabulary, teach concepts, and offer them your own enthusiasm for life. It is this enthusiasm for what you see, hear, and feel and for the everyday challenges and joys of life that will help them love learning for the rest of their lives.

—Marilyn Grevstad

How It Feels to Be a Parent of a Preschooler

Raising a child of this age is a highly emotional experience. One parent wrote this, for example:

I am a parent of a four-and-a-half-year-old, and I experience a *buffet of emotions* toward him every day.

My child's changeable nature is very *challenging* to deal with. You never know when you might say or do the wrong thing! His resulting explosiveness can be very *exasperating*. He tests my patience with demands, rigidity, noisy teasing, and nonstop activity that easily gets "out of bounds." Sometimes I feel so *weary*.

On the other hand, I *love* the *fun* we have. I *delight* in his silliness in play and language and in the places his imagination has taken us. I feel *tenderness* and *warmth* for my boy during moments when he is eager to please and to be sweet and affectionate. I have learned that I can encourage this behavior by giving him the opportunity to think and cooperate in his own time. It's *exciting* to watch him grow at his own rate.

—Sue Hansen

Where to Go for Additional Support

If you have tried the ideas in the Suggestion Circles, talked with your family and friends, read some child-rearing books, and still feel stuck with a problem, here are some places to call for additional help or to find out about parenting classes. If you have difficulty finding a telephone number after looking in both the white and the yellow pages, call any of these sources and ask them to help you find the number you need.

Community Services

Crisis or hot-line numbers
YMCA, YWCA, or a local church or synagogue
Parents Without Partners International
Chemical abuse treatment centers
Chemical abuse prevention programs
Community civic centers
Women's or men's support groups
Battered women's and children's shelters
Planned Parenthood and other family planning
   centers
Alcoholics Anonymous
Parents Anonymous
Sexual assault centers
Local hospitals

Private Services

Psychologists, social workers, psychiatrists, therapists, family counselors

Schools

Community education (local school district)
Colleges or universities
Community colleges
Vocational and technical schools

Government

Community mental health services
Public health nurse or department
Child protection services
Family service agencies
County social service agencies

Interview the persons who will help you to see if they know about the area in which you need help. If you don't get the help you need, go somewhere else until you do.

—The Editors

How to Lead a Suggestion Circle

The Suggestion Circle is an efficient tool for collecting a variety of ideas for solving problems. It is the opposite of brainstorming.

As the Suggestion Circle leader, do this:

1. Ask people to sit in a circle.
2. Tell the person who has the problem to be the "listener" and to state the problem clearly and concisely. The group may ask clarifying questions.
3. Ask the person to listen to each suggestion with no comment other than "thank you."
4. Ask a group member to make a written list of the suggestions. This will allow the person to give full attention to listening to the suggestions.
5. Ask the group members to think of their best solution to the problem. Ask them to state their suggestions in one or two sentences. They are not to comment on or evaluate each other's suggestions. Go around the Circle.
6. When everyone has had a chance to give a suggestion, hand the written list of suggestions to the person with the problem. He or she can use it as a resource in deciding what to do.

A Suggestion Circle of twelve people takes five minutes to complete. It is fast, caring, and efficient, and it honors everyone in the group.

A Suggestion Circle can also be done by telephone.

1. When you have a problem that you need help with, phone six friends.
2. Clearly and quickly explain the problem to each friend, and ask for his or her best suggestion. Writing the problem out before you call may help you state it more clearly.
3. Listen to the suggestion and write it down.
4. Do not comment on the suggestion, other than to say "thank you."
5. After you have phoned each friend, look over your list of suggestions and decide which to use. Acknowledge the support that you have received from your friends.

—Sandra Sittko

Conclusion

As we worked on this project over the past two years, it became very apparent that our meetings were providing much more than material for a book. The sharing we have done and the support and nurturance we had given each other at our different stages of parenting has been invaluable. One of us adopted three children during this time, another gave birth, and another became pregnant and gave birth. Two of us have older children—some just leaving home. It has been a very rich and full time.

Our children are growing wonders, and they continually insist that we grow in ways we never imagined possible. This book and the others in this series have shown us that, as parents, we all have much to offer each other. The pages of this book are full of solutions to common concerns about children three to six years old, offered by hundreds of parents as varied as are the suggestions.

Since we want the best for ourselves and our families, we have helped one another find new ways to solve problems. We offer this book for you to use as your family grows and changes. You can trust your inner wisdom to know what you need. And affirm yourself for being the resourceful, caring parent that you are. Your children are very lucky to have you!

—Melanie Weiss

Resources

Books for Adults

Alexander, Josi, et al. *Is My Baby OK? Toilet Training*. (Audiotape) Los Angeles: PIPS Parent House, Inc., 1983.

Ames, Louise B., and Haber, Carol Chase. *He Hit Me First: When Brothers and Sisters Fight*. New York: Dembner Books, 1982.

Ames, Louise B., and Ilg, Frances L. *Your Five Year Old: Sunny and Serene*. New York: Dell, 1981.

_____. *Your Four Year Old: Wild and Wonderful*. New York: Dell, 1980.

_____. *Your Three Year Old: Friend or Enemy*. New York: Dell, 1980.

Barrow, Cheryl, and Scheezer, Cathy. *Great Parties for Young Children*. New York: Walker and Co., 1981.

Beall, Pamela, and Nipp, Susan. *Wee Sing Play Book and Cassette*. Los Angeles, Calif.: Price/Stern/Sloan, 1982.

Bozarth-Campbell, Alla. *Life Is Goodbye—Life Is Hello: Grieving Well Through All Kinds of Loss*. Minneapolis: CompCare Publications, 1982.

Calladine, Carole and Andrew. *Raising Brothers and Sisters Without Raising the Roof*. Minneapolis: Winston Press, 1983.

Cherry, Clare. *Parents, Please Don't Sit on Your Children*. Belmont, Calif.: Pitman Books, 1985.

Clarke, Jean Illsley. *Self-Esteem: A Family Affair*. Minneapolis: Winston Press, Inc., 1978.

Crary, Elizabeth. *Without Spanking or Spoiling*. Seattle: Parenting Press, 1979.

————. *Kids Can Cooperate*. Seattle: Parenting Press, 1984.

Dads Only (Monthly periodical). Julian, Calif.: Paul Lewis.

Elkind, David. *The Hurried Child: Growing Up Too Fast Too Soon*. Washington, D.C.: Addison-Wesley, 1981.

Family Pastimes Catalogue. Perth, Ontario, Canada K7H 3C6. Family Pastimes Yearly Catalogue.

Fluegelman, Andrew. *The New Games Book*. San Francisco: The Headlands Press, 1976.

Fraiberg, Selma. *The Magic Years: Understanding and Handling the Problems of Early Childhood*. New York: Doubleday, 1984.

Hart-Rossi, Janie. *Protect Your Child from Sexual Abuse*. Seattle: Parenting Press, 1983.

Hendricks, Gay. *The Centering Book*. Englewood Cliffs, N.J.: Prentice-Hall, Inc., 1975.

He Told Me Not to Tell. Renton, Wash.: King County Rape Relief, 1979.

Ilg, Frances L., and Ames, Louise B. *Child Behavior*. New York: Harper & Row, 1955.

Kelly, Marguerite, and Parsons, Elia S. *The Mother's Almanac*. New York: Doubleday, 1975.

Lansky, Vicki. *Practical Parenting Tips*. Deephaven, Minn.: Meadowbrook Press, 1981.

Lappe, Frances M. *Diet for a Small Planet*. New York: Ballantine Books, Inc., 1975.

Levin, Pamela. *Becoming the Way We Are*. Wenatchee, Wash.: Directed Media, Inc., 1974.

McCullough, Bonnie, and Monson, Susan. *Four Hundred-One Ways to Get Your Kids to Work at Home*. New York: St. Martin's Press, Inc., 1982.

Mercer Island Preschool Association. *Rainy Day Activities for Preschoolers*. Mercer Island, Wash.: Mercer Island Preschool Association, 1983.

Pappas, Michael G. *Prime Time for Families*. Minneapolis: Winston Press, 1980.

Pogrebin, Letty C. *Growing Up Free*. New York: Bantam Books, Inc., 1981.

Riley, Sue S. *How to Generate Values in Young Children*. Washington, D.C.: National Association for the Education of Young Children, 1984.

Satir, Virginia. *Peoplemaking*. Palo Alto, Calif.: Science and Behavior Books, Inc., 1972.

Segal, Marilyn, and Adcock, Don. *Just Pretending: Ways to Help Children Grow Through Their Own Imaginative Play*. Englewood Cliffs, N.J.: Prentice-Hall, Inc., 1981.

Trelease, Jim. *The Read-Aloud Handbook*. New York: Penguin Books, 1982.

Winn, Marie. *The Plug-In Drug*. New York: Viking-Penguin, 1977.

Zimbardo, Phillip G., and Radl, Shirley L. *The Shy Child: A Parent's Guide to Preventing and*

Overcoming Shyness from Infancy to Adulthood. New York: McGraw-Hill, 1981.

Books for Children

Ancona, George. *Bodies.* New York: E. P. Dutton, 1973.

_____. *I Feel: A Picture Book of Emotions.* New York: E. P. Dutton, 1977.

Berenstain, Stan and Jan. *The Berenstain Bears' Moving Day.* New York: Random House, 1981.

_____. *The Berenstain Bears and the Messy Room.* New York: Random House, 1983.

_____. *The Berenstain Bears and Too Much TV.* New York: Random House, 1984.

Brown, Margaret W. *The Dead Bird.* Reading, Mass.: Addison-Wesley, 1958.

Crary, Elizabeth. *I Can't Wait.* Seattle: Parenting Press, 1982.

_____. *I Want It.* Seattle: Parenting Press, 1982.

_____. *I Want to Play.* Seattle: Parenting Press, 1982.

_____. *My Name Is Not Dummy.* Seattle: Parenting Press, 1983.

Cross, Laurella B. *Jenny's New Game.* Roswell, N. Mex.: L. B. Cross, 1984.

Dayee, Frances S. *Private Zone: A Read-Together Book to Help Parents Help Children Deal with and Prevent Sexual Assault.* New York: Warner Books, Inc., 1982.

DePaola, Tomie. *Nana Upstairs and Nana Downstairs.* New York: Penguin Books, 1978.

_____. *The Knight and Dragon.* New York: G. P. Putnam's Sons, 1980.

Freed, Alvyn. *TA for Tots.* Rolling Hills Estate, Calif.: Jalmar Press, 1973.

Freeman, Lory. *It's My Body.* Seattle: Parenting Press, 1983.

Kaufman, Joe. *How We Are Born, How We Grow, How Our Bodies Work, and How We Learn.* New York: Golden Press, 1975.

Mayle, Peter. *Where Did I Come From?* Secaucus, N.J.: Lyle Stuart, Inc., 1973.

Meyer, Linda D. *Safety Zone: A Book Teaching Children Abduction Prevention Skills.* Philadelphia: Franklin Institute Press, 1984.

Miller, J. P. *Tales from Aesop.* New York: Random House, 1976.

O'Callahan, Jay. *The Little Dragon and Other Stories.* (Storytelling Tape) 90 Old Mount Skirgo Road, Marshfield, Mass. 02050.

Steiner, Claude. *Warm Fuzzy Tale.* Rolling Hills Estate, Calif.: Jalmar Press, 1977.

Wood, Audrey (Illus.). *Quick as a Cricket.* Sudbury, Mass.: Playspaces International, 1982.

About the Editors

Jean Illsley Clarke is the author of the book *Self-Esteem: A Family Affair* and of the parenting program of the same name. Jean is a Transactional Analyst, a parent educator, is married and the mother of three. She holds a Master of Arts in Human Development and an honorary Doctor of Human Services. She loves to play imaginary games with children this age.

Marilyn Grevstad is most often found surrounded by children. She is a parent educator for Shoreline Community College in Seattle. She directs the North City Cooperative Preschool where parents and their infants, toddlers, and preschoolers learn together. She and her husband, Ben, are the parents of four young men, Kris, Kurt, Hans, and Nels and one young woman, Fritzi. Marilyn facilitates "Self-Esteem: A Family Affair" classes.

Sue Hansen, B.A., was a strawberry farmer until her first child was born, then she discovered she was far more interested in his growth than in raising strawberries. She and her husband, Don, are the parents of Jacob, age five, and five-month-old Elizabeth. Sue is a facilitator of "Self-Esteem: A Family Affair" parenting classes and is working toward certification to become a La Leche League leader. Her love of dance and physical fitness keeps her steadily enrolled in Jazzercise classes.

Mary Sleeth Paananen, R.N., B.S., is a mother, facilitator of "Self-Esteem: A Family Affair" classes, and a registered nurse (BSM). While Mary was working on this book, she, husband Terry, and son William, five years, were joined through adoption by Jon, six years, Jeff, four years, and Erin, three years. One of Mary's strengths is her ability to network and use resources. Their preschool family friends and neighboring families (with fifteen children under eight years old) are a constant source of "Whys," "Try this," and "Ahas!" Before William was born, Mary worked with multiply handicapped children and their families, not only helping tend to their medical needs but also to their supportive and nurturing needs.

Melanie Weiss, M.Ed., has been an art teacher, has worked with residents in a psychiatric hospital, has done volunteer work with Child Protective Services, and is a trained facilitator of "Self-Esteem: A Family Affair" parenting classes. She and her husband, Ron, are the parents of Eli, Adam, and Evan. Since having her first, she has been primarily a mother at home, and believes there is no greater vehicle for our own growth than our children.

Index

133

Other Learning Materials Available

Developmental Tapes, by Jean Illsley Clarke. These audio cassette tapes present important information about children and the nurturing they need. Told in entertaining and easy-to-understand language from the perspective of children of different ages, the tapes describe child care by parents and by day-care providers. The stories allow adults to set aside fear or guilt and have the distance they may need to hear the information presented. The tapes, told in both male and female voices, are also useful tools for helping older children understand their little brother's and sister's needs and behavior. Each story is twelve-to-eighteen minutes long; at least eight spaced listenings are recommended.

Ups and Downs with Feelings, by Carole Gesme. This collection of games features a game board with a wide variety of "feeling faces" to help children and adults identify feelings and learn ways to be responsible for them. Included are directions for seven separate games, one of which uses the affirmations printed in this book.

Affirmation Cards. Tiny colored cards, with a separate affirmation printed on each, that can be read, carried, or given as gifts.

For more information, including prices, write to

Daisy Press
16535 Ninth Avenue North
Plymouth, MN 55447